Jᴀᴍᴇs Fᴀʟʟᴏᴡs

BLIND INTO BAGHDAD

Jᴀᴍᴇs Fᴀʟʟᴏᴡs is *The Atlantic Monthly*'s national correspondent and has worked for the magazine for more than twenty years. He is a former editor of *US News & World Report* and a former chief White House speechwriter for Jimmy Carter. His previous books include *Breaking the News: How the Media Undermine American Democracy*, *Free Flight*, *Looking at the Sun*, *More Like Us*, and *National Defense*, which won the American Book Award for nonfiction. He has been a finalist for the National Magazine Award four times, and his article about the consequences of victory in Iraq, "The Fifty-First State?" won that award in 2003.

BLIND INTO BAGHDAD

AMERICA'S WAR IN IRAQ

JAMES FALLOWS

VINTAGE BOOKS

A Division of Random House, Inc.

New York

The articles in this collection were previously published in *The Atlantic Monthly:*

"The Fifty-First State?" (November 2002)
"Blind into Baghdad" (January/February 2004)
"Bush's Lost Year" (October 2004)
"Will Iran Be Next?" (December 2004)
"Why Iraq Has No Army" (December 2005)

Library of Congress Cataloging-in-Publication Data
Fallows, James, M.
Blind into Baghdad : America's war in Iraq / James Fallows.—1st ed.
p. cm.
1. Iraq War, 2003–.   2. Iraq War, 2003—Diplomatic history.
3. United States—Military policy.   I. Title.
DS79.76.F3487 2006
956.7044'3—dc22
2006046110

Vintage ISBN-10: 0-307-27796-8
Vintage ISBN-13: 978-0-307-27796-1

Author photograph © Deborah Fallows
Book design by R. Bull

www.vintagebooks.com

Printed in the United States of America
10   9   8   7   6   5   4   3   2   1

For Cullen Murphy

CONTENTS

INTRODUCTION

Most of the material in this book first appeared as articles in *The Atlantic Monthly* between 2002 and 2005. When time they were written, the articles illustrated two of the ways a monthly magazine, with its very long lead time, can attempt to cover major news stories that are being reported nonstop and almost instantaneously over TV and radio, in blogs, and by leading newspapers.

One approach is anticipation. This involves choosing an upcoming event when it is still too far away for other media to have turned to it and laying out a way of thinking about the event that might affect other coverage, and thereby help shape public attitudes, when the right time comes. The other is reconstruction—pulling together details, comparing accounts, answering leftover questions, and ultimately retelling a story that was misexplained or only half explained before. Like all of journalism, which is defined as the best version of the truth that is available by deadline time, magazine articles are imperfect. Like most acts of prediction, the anticipatory articles are even more obviously imperfect than the reconstructions, which were written with the advantage of knowing how things turned out. Yet as the events described here move from the realm of current events into history, the reports in this book are meant to show the value of both anticipation and reconstruction in understanding major changes in national and international life.

The subject of the book is America's preparation for and conduct of its war in Iraq, whose combat phase began in March 2003. Because that war played so large a part in the U.S. government response to the terrorist attacks of September 11, 2001, assessing the war naturally raises questions about the wisdom, competence, and effectiveness of the overall American strategy against Islamic terrorism.

The cumulative argument of the book is that this strategy was gravely flawed in both design and execution. This is not a partisan judgment, in that it does not claim that Republicans made mistakes that Democrats would have avoided. It is impossible to know how a President Al Gore would have responded to the 9/11 attacks or what a President John Kerry could have done about political and military problems in an Iraq already occupied by U.S. troops. (One of the reasons it is hard to know these things is that the Democrats have been so hesitant and internally divided about presenting an alternative plan for Iraq in particular and national security strategy in general.) All we know for sure is what George W. Bush and his administration chose to do, and not do, in the name of protecting their country—and those choices, which constituted U.S. national policy in the early part of the twenty-first century, are the ones assessed in this book.

What the administration "should have" known about Iraq as it prepared to invade is the theme of the first two chapters. "The Fifty-First State" was officially published in the *Atlantic*'s November 2002 issue, but it was put up on the magazine's Web site as soon as it was finished, in August of that year, in the hope that its argument would be considered during the intensifying debate about whether and when to go to war. The article was an explicit act of anticipation.

Cullen Murphy, the *Atlantic*'s managing editor at the time (and the guiding force behind all of the articles collected here), made a journalistic bet in the spring of 2002. Warfare was winding down in Afghanistan, and officially nothing had been decided about carrying the battle to Iraq, but all the unofficial signs pointed toward a showdown.

To give a few examples from my own experience: The phones at my home and office in Washington, DC, were out of service all day long on September 11, 2001. The very next day, one of the first people I reached for an interview was James Woolsey, who had directed the CIA early in Bill Clinton's administration and who later in the administration had signed statements calling for the removal of Saddam Hussein. "We don't know where this attack came from," Woolsey told me while ruins were still smoking in New York and Washington (as I mention in the second chapter of this book). "But the response has to involve Iraq"—by which he meant not that blame had somehow to be pinned on Saddam Hussein but instead that the United States had to go to the root of its long-term problems in the Middle East, which to Woolsey and others of similar outlook meant Iraq.

A few days later, I interviewed a former Air Force fighter pilot who was working on post-9/11 retaliatory strategy at the Pentagon. Like many other Americans, he suggested that the attacks were this era's counterparts to Pearl Harbor. But to him that comparison underscored the importance of taking the fight to Iraq. "Even though the [Pearl Harbor] attack came from Japan, FDR concentrated on beating the Nazis first," he said, since Hitler posed the graver threat. In this man's view, Saddam Hussein's role was comparable to Hitler's after Pearl Harbor. His regime in Iraq might or might not eventually prove to have had anything to do with the destruction of the World Trade Center. But since he was, from this perspective, the most oppressive tyrant in the Arab world and the most influential potential sponsor of future terrorists, any "solution" that left him in power would be no solution at all. I heard similar thoughts, with greater emphasis on the transformative benefits of bringing democracy to Iraq, a few months later from Deputy Secretary of Defense Paul Wolfowitz in his Pentagon office. Everyone operating in Washington was receiving comparable signals.

If war with Iraq seemed increasingly likely within a few months of the 9/11 attacks, U.S. victory in such a war seemed absolutely certain. The United States (albeit with numerous allies) had humiliated Iraq's forces a dozen years earlier, in the first Gulf War. Since then, American troops, weapons, and strategies had all improved, and Iraq's had all gotten worse. And so—to return to the journalistic decision—early in 2002 Cullen Murphy recognized that America would sooner or later have challenged Iraq's forces—and defeated them. Our journalistic opportunity was to ask: What then? My role was to explore this question in Washington, while, at different times, Michael Kelly, Robert Kaplan, William

Langewiesche, and Mark Bowden reported from Iraq. (Kelly, who had been the *Atlantic*'s editor from the fall of 1999 through the fall of 2002, joined the U.S. Army's Third Infantry Division in early 2003 as an embedded reporter for the *Atlantic*. On April 3, 2003, during the division's drive toward Baghdad early in the war, Kelly was killed in a Humvee incident, along with two soldiers in the same vehicle.)

I spent several months in the spring and summer of 2002 interviewing people whose experience and expertise prepared them to discuss the likely consequences of victory over Iraq. These were mainly people who had served in or studied other American occupations—of Germany, Japan, the Balkans, Haiti, Korea, even the Philippines after the Spanish-American War. In addition I met with people who were experts in Iraq's history, society, and economy, and those who had prepared estimates of what would happen when the lid of oppression was finally removed.

From these conversations emerged surprisingly consistent themes: how long and difficult, as opposed to quick and easy, an occupation was likely to be; how important sectional and religious differences within Iraq would probably become; and how crucial it was for the new occupying power to ensure, from the very start, that a majority of Iraqis could see the benefits of an improved daily life, through physical security, a restored economy, and such mundane features as reliable electricity and water supplies.

I reported these findings, and others, in "The Fifty-First State." The title was meant to suggest the long-term responsibilities America would take on if it invaded Iraq. "The day after a war ended, Iraq would become America's problem," the article said. "Because we would have destroyed the political order and done physical damage in the process, the claims on American resources and attention would be comparable to those of any U.S. state. Conquered Iraqis would turn to the U.S. government for emergency relief, civil order, economic reconstruction, and protection of their borders."

In the process of reporting and writing that article, it naturally affected my own view of the war that was about to begin. Like most people in America, I wholeheartedly supported the campaign against the Taliban in Afghanistan in the six months after the 9/11 attacks. This was the regime that had sheltered Osama bin Laden, in addition to dragging its own people, especially women, into premodern misery. No one seriously challenged America's right to retaliate for the grievous wound it had endured, nor the fundamental justice of an anti-Taliban campaign. In addition to having a clear political, even moral, basis, the war in Afghanistan was also prudently managed. American forces were able to work with a diverse group of international allies, and to leave much of the ground combat to Afghan forces of the Northern Alliance. By invading Afghanistan, the United States certainly took on some responsibility for helping rehabilitate the country. But neither America's leaders nor those of liberated Afghanistan claimed that the United States would now make beleaguered, xenophobic Afghanistan into a showpiece of democracy, or that the new Afghan example would help transform the Middle East.

Iraq was something else altogether. I was not axiomatically against using American troops to force regime change there. *The Atlantic Monthly* itself had published Mark Bowden's "Tales of the Tyrant," an influential chronicle of the ways and means of Saddam Hussein's oppression, in May 2002. Michael Kelly, the *Atlantic*'s editor at the time, had in his book *Martyr's Day* written about Saddam's massacre of rebellious Shiites after the first Gulf War. Kelly never lost his moral certainty that such a monster must be opposed and ultimately removed. I lacked Kelly's standing as firsthand witness to Saddam Hussein's brutality. But of course I felt that if such a tyrant could be driven from power in a way consistent with America's larger and longer-term interests in the world, then America should do it.

The problem was the alignment with America's broadest interests. The evil of a foreign leader has never settled the question of whether the United States should intervene to remove him; it merely opens the question. And unless the nation is fighting for its absolute survival, or is being run by absolutists who view foreign policy as a crusade, the subsequent debate turns on practicalities. What would it take to remove the evildoer? How many risks and commitments is the nation willing to accept, and how much evil is it willing to inflict, along the way, to accomplish the goal?

On these practical grounds, I opposed the decision to go to war. If evidence finally emerged to suggest that Iraq's weapons posed a real, immediate threat, America could act at that time—as it would against any other peril. Until then, it seemed to me, the United States had far more to gain by waiting than by striking before it absolutely had to. With

UN inspectors crawling over Iraq, Saddam Hussein was unlikely to get a new weapons program going quickly or by surprise. Therefore time was on America's side. At least in principle, the United States could use the passing months to broaden its coalition against Saddam Hussein, or at least reduce outright opposition from many of its allies. If and when it eventually went to war, it might have been better prepared to win the war—and the peace. It could conceivably find a way to attract some Islamic or Arabic-speaking forces to its side. It could prepare more thoroughly for the occupation. If the thing had to be done, it might as well be done right. If America chose not to go to war today, it could always reverse that choice tomorrow. But on the day it went to war, its course would be set for years to come.

In those last few weeks before the invasion, some proponents of the war made their own practical arguments. The troops were in place; they couldn't be kept there indefinitely. The summer was coming, and after a while it would be too hot to fight in the desert in those bulky suits designed to protect soldiers against nerve gas, germs, or radiation. The status quo was forcing hardship on the Iraqi populace, which was suffering because of economic sanctions, and was also wearing out the U.S. military, as it flew daily patrols over Iraq's extensive "no-fly" zones. Compared with all this, evicting Saddam and taking over Iraq would surely be a "cakewalk," in the words of Kenneth Adelman, an arms control official in the Reagan administration (and a longtime friend of mine).

I disagreed with hawks in and around the Bush administration for many reasons. Everything I had heard in the months of working on this first article convinced me that the war and its aftermath would be no cakewalk. Everything I had learned in twenty-five years of covering military and political affairs sobered me about the unforeseen consequences of any decision to go to war. Yes, delaying a war meant leaving a dictator in power with consequent suffering for many people in Iraq. But we had no good idea of what kind of suffering would follow a war. Even taken at face value, the administration's report about WMD (weapons of mass destruction) threats from Iraq did not mean America *had* to attack immediately, in my view. And if it did not have to attack, then it should not go ahead, not simply because of the complications within Iraq itself but because the way a war would inevitably suck time, money, and attention from every other aspect of a "war on terror."

Even at the time, I had indications of a point that seems all too obvious in retrospect. Before the war, it was hard to draw administration officials into any serious discussion of what would happen the day after Baghdad fell. One reason, it now seems evident, is that the likely answers to that question would be so troubling as to make the entire prospect of war less appealing. Some members of the administration had probably convinced themselves that getting out of Iraq would be nearly as quick and easy as getting in. The more serious and senior members probably sensed that governing Iraq could be complicated. But that was a problem they were willing to face later on, once they had dealt with the more urgent problem (in their minds) of getting rid of Saddam Hussein. I give an early indication of this outlook on page 7 of this book.

I also disagreed with the "liberal hawks" who thought that this exercise of American power would be in the finest tradition of America's role and responsibility as a liberator. My reaction was like that of a traditional conservative, when hearing the latest liberal scheme to reform human nature. It sounds great in theory, but isn't it likely to end in tears? The scholars, strategists, and military historians I interviewed when working on this article stressed how difficult, demanding, and uncertain would be the course of creating a new, unified, democratic Iraq. This is not a role at which America excels—unless forced into such duty, as it was after World War II. Many liberals felt it would be better to try despite the uncertainties. I was apprehensive about what the attempt would mean, unless America were truly prepared for the many years of commitment involved.

This may sound like a hairsplitting set of distinctions, but I set them out here in order to explain my outlook as the war drew near. If it had been up to me, the United States would have kept waiting—and preparing, and building its coalition, and applying pressure—until it was forced to go to war. But it was not up to me. My country was going to war. Therefore by early 2003 my own argument shifted. I spent less time discussing whether or not there should be a war—and more emphasizing that the United States must do everything possible to make the war and its aftermath a success.

Six months after "The Fifty-First State" was published, as the difficulties of governing postwar Iraq were becoming too obvious to ignore, the article received the National Magazine Award. Some of the specific warnings and details in it have not stood up well. There were no mass refugee flows of Iraqis after the war—largely because there were no chemical or biological attacks to provoke an exodus. Managing or forgiving Iraq's foreign debt, which many people had worried about before the war, proved to be a relatively minor problem. The rules of thumb I offered in the article for deciding how many foreign troops it would take to ensure order in Iraq turned out to be low.

But many other specific warnings offered by my sources did prove to be well-founded. And the basic point of the article—that by conquering a country in a discretionary war the United States would shoulder vast and unpredictable responsibilities—certainly held up. A British intelligence official whom I quoted but who would not let me use his name said that the dreams of easily implanting democracy on Iraq's soil were "the ruminations of insane people." This sounded rash, but such cautions about the disappointments ahead in Iraq stood up better than the administration's assurances of how American troops would be received.

I would like to pretend otherwise, but the warnings in the article had not been very difficult for me to collect. I simply telephoned and visited people and asked their views. I was not an expert on Iraq or the Middle East, and I was working from strictly nonclassified sources. Surely the U.S. government itself had vastly more detailed and incisive analyses to work from—or so its citizens would hope. As it turns out, the government was in fact very well informed about what lay ahead. Where the prewar predictions I had collected proved to be true in general but off in a few particulars, the government's own efforts, not publicized at the time, proved unnervingly correct.

The second chapter of this book, "Blind into Baghdad," makes clear exactly how well informed the government was. I did interviews for the article in the summer and fall of 2003, and it was published at the end of that year. The article was an effort to deal with the problems of postwar Iraq, not through anticipation but through journalistic reconstruction. Before the war, it looked as if the occupation would be troublesome; soon after the war, the United States appeared to have been utterly surprised by challenges it ought to have foreseen. How could this be?

The big surprise to me in reporting this article was that many organizations both inside and outside the U.S. government had in fact anticipated almost every difficulty that later arose in Iraq, and suggested measures to offset it. After the article appeared some members of the administration told me that it was unfair—worse, naive—to make this point. It is the nature of a bureaucracy to warn about absolutely everything, they said. Presidents and cabinet secretaries learn that they must look past this cover-your-ass protective instinct from careerists if they want to get anything done.

But as it turns out, the warnings were something more than hypercautious boilerplate. All of the major institutions that would later play a role in the occupation—the military, the intelligence agencies, the State Department, plus a number of nongovernmental bodies—were doing everything they could to forestall problems they saw developing. "The administration will be admired in retrospect for how much knowledge it created about the challenge it was taking on" in Iraq, the article said. "But the administration will be condemned for what it did with what was known. The problems the United States has encountered are precisely the ones its own expert agencies warned against. Exactly what went wrong with the occupation will be studied for years—or should be."

Two other chapters are reconstructions that try to explain other significant policy failures. "Why Iraq Has No Army" is an extension of the reasoning behind "Blind into Baghdad." By the time that article was published, in December 2005, there were indications that American efforts to create and train a native Iraqi security force were improving as the U.S. military learned from past mistakes. But there was no way to be sure that the training process was getting better as fast as the threat from Iraq's insurgents was getting worse. Nor was it obvious why Americans wasted so much time before they got serious about training Iraqis. The answers to these questions affected all parties to the Iraq debate inside the United States. Those who opposed the war and wanted U.S. troops to leave, those who supported it but were concerned about mounting protests in both America and Iraq, those in the U.S. military who were alarmed about the wear and tear created by long deployments in Iraq—all shared an interest in enabling Iraqi soldiers to replace Americans as quickly as possible.

The story of why it didn't happen is a specific case of the

general problems of the occupation. That is, it involved unrealistic expectations before the assault on Baghdad; crucial missteps in the first days and weeks after Saddam Hussein's government fell; a delayed adaptation to worsening circumstances; and an improved approach that may have come too late.

The other chapter about Iraq, first published in the fall of 2004 as "Bush's Lost Year," is the one whose process of reportage was most sobering for me. The idea behind this article was to reconstruct exactly how the general need to respond to the 9/11 attacks had been transformed into the specific need to invade Iraq. Through the process of interviews and research, I became convinced that the early months of 2002 were the real watershed in American policy, even more than the weeks immediately after September 11, 2001, had been. At the beginning of 2002, the government of the United States knew that it faced a huge challenge in dealing with Islamic terrorism—but it also had tremendous resources to draw on and almost unlimited options from which to choose. Its federal budget was still running a surplus; its military had barely been strained by its combat in Afghanistan; the sympathy and support of most of the world gave it "soft power" reinforcement for its exercise of hard, military power.

By the end of that year, America's international ambitions focused almost exclusively on removing Saddam Hussein. Its military was becoming overcommitted; its budget had begun the dramatic shift toward chronic deficits; international opinion had largely turned against it. This shift, I ended up believing, was a dramatic and historic mistake for the United States, because of the many avenues of response it closed off: using resources for homeland security, finishing the battle in Afghanistan in the right way, and building a large alliance against Islamic extremism, and because it overtaxed the military in a way that made its limits obvious.

It is conceivable that the ultimate judgment will be the reverse—that Iraq could turn out so well, and with such a broad ripple effect, that forcing regime change there eventually seems worth every foregone opportunity. At certain points since the American intervention in Iraq, positive developments in Syria, Lebanon, and elsewhere have seemed to indicate that the removal of Saddam Hussein might indeed be the start of a democratic trend throughout the Arab-Islamic world. But at the time of my reporting the "Lost Year" article in 2004, and of this writing two years later, very few people I have encountered at working levels of the nation's security establishment believe or expect that the ripple effects of Iraq will be mainly positive in the foreseeable future. Shifting from an effort against terrorism in general, to a campaign against Saddam Hussein in particular, was the decision—the historic gamble—on which George W. Bush staked his reputation and the nation's welfare. Evidence available as I write suggest that it was the wrong choice.

The final chapter is once more an exercise in anticipation. It appeared in the *Atlantic* just after the 2004 presidential election, but it went to press before the winner in that election was known. Therefore it dealt with a problem sure to face either a reelected President Bush or a newly elected

President Kerry: how to deal with Iran's quest for nuclear weapons. The tool our magazine chose for anticipation was one we had never tried before. We sponsored a "war game," which in military parlance can mean a full-scale, expensive exercise with troops and tanks but which usually means a role-playing exercise or thought experiment, to see how parties to a conflict will respond. Our game examined the consequences of a preemptive strike on Iranian facilities by American or Israeli warplanes. The conclusions indicated that American leaders should think very, very carefully before initiating such an attack, more carefully than they had before invading Iraq.

I would like to note here my sincere gratitude to Cullen Murphy, who served as managing editor of *The Atlantic Monthly* from 1985 to 2005. It is because he provided the original idea for each of the articles collected here, as well as because of his influence on *The Atlantic Monthly* over the last two decades, that this book is dedicated to him. Michael Kelly, under whose leadership I rejoined the *Atlantic* in 2000 after several years away, disagreed with much of what I thought and wrote about Iraq. But he supported publication of "The Fifty-First State," the only one of these articles to appear before his death, and his example of courage, independent thinking, personal loyalty, and joyous living inspired everyone at the magazine during the three years he led it. I am grateful to Corby Kummer, Sue Parilla, and Martha Spaulding, who edited, fact-checked, and improved the articles. Scott Stossel, Toby Lester, Yvonne Rolzhausen, and many others in the *Atlantic*'s Boston office worked non-stop to make the magazine and its writers look as good as possible. Mary Parsons, the *Atlantic*'s art director when these articles appeared, presented them with striking images, including the photo that is also used with a different cropping on this book's cover. David Bradley, owner and chairman of the *Atlantic* since 1999, generously and patiently provided the resources that made this reporting possible; John Galloway, president of Atlantic Media, and John Fox Sullivan, our group publisher, provided constant support and encouragement. The magazine's publisher, Elizabeth Baker Keffer, and her colleagues on the *Atlantic*'s business staff have worked tirelessly to expand the magazine's reach and influence. I am also grateful to the *Atlantic*'s management for its generous policy of assigning writers copyright to their articles, which allows me to present this collection.

Since part of the purpose of this book is to present real-time assessments of history as it unfolded, I have left these articles as they were originally published. In a few places I have added footnotes to mention recent changes in events, or to provide the answers to questions that were still left open when the articles were first published.

Washington, DC
April 2006

THE FIFTY-FIRST STATE?

Through the summer of 2002 I interviewed several dozen people about what could be expected in Iraq after the United States dislodged Saddam Hussein. An assumption behind the question was that sooner or later the United States would go to war—and would go with at best a fraction of the support it enjoyed eleven years ago when fighting Iraq during the Gulf War. Most nations in the region and traditional U.S. allies would be neutral or hostile unless the Bush administration could present new evidence of imminent danger from Iraq.

A further assumption was that even alone, U.S. forces would win this war. The victory might be slower than in the last war against Iraq, and it would certainly cost more American lives.* But in the end U.S. tanks, attack airplanes,

---

*This is a reminder of the risks of saying "certainly" about anything that has not yet occurred. Although Operation Iraqi Freedom, which began in March 2003, and the subsequent occupation will ultimately claim many more lives than Operation Desert Storm in 1991, the initial casualty levels were very similar. By most accounts, the United States suffered 148 battle deaths during the entirety of Operation Desert Storm. During the main

precision-guided bombs, special-operations forces, and other assets would crush the Iraqi military. The combat phase of the war would be over when the United States destroyed Saddam Hussein's control over Iraq's government, armed forces, and stockpile of weapons.

What then?

The people I asked were spies, Arabists, oil-company officials, diplomats, scholars, policy experts, and many active-duty and retired soldiers. They were from the United States, Europe, and the Middle East. Some firmly supported a preemptive war against Iraq; more were opposed. As of late summer, before the serious domestic debate had begun, most of the people I spoke with expected a war to occur.

I began my research sharing the view, prevailing in Washington through 2002, that forcing "regime change" on Iraq was our era's grim historical necessity: starting a war would be bad, but waiting to have war brought to us would be worse. This view depended to some degree on trusting that the U.S. government had information not available to the public about exactly how close Saddam Hussein was to having usable nuclear warheads or other weapons of mass destruction. It also drew much of its power from an analogy every member of the public could understand—to Nazi Germany. In retrospect, the only sin in resisting Hitler had been waiting too long. Thus would it be in dealing with Saddam Hus-

---

battle stage of Operation Iraqi Freedom, in March and April of 2003, the United States suffered 138 battle deaths. Within the next three years, of course, well over two thousand additional Americans had died in Iraq.

sein today. Richard Perle, a Reagan-era Defense Department official who is one of the most influential members outside government of what is frequently called the "war party," expressed this thought in representative form in an August column for the London *Daily Telegraph*: "A preemptive strike against Hitler at the time of Munich would have meant an immediate war, as opposed to the one that came later. Later was much worse."

Nazi and Holocaust analogies have a trumping power in many arguments, and their effect in Washington was to make doubters seem weak—Neville Chamberlains versus the Winston Churchills who were ready to face the truth. The most experienced military figure in the Bush cabinet, Secretary of State Colin Powell, was cast as the main "wet," because of his obvious discomfort with an effort that few allies would support. His instincts fit the general sociology of the Iraq debate: As a rule, the strongest advocates of preemptive attack, within the government and in the press, had neither served in the military nor lived in Arab societies. Military veterans and Arabists were generally doves. For example: Paul Wolfowitz, the deputy secretary of defense and the intellectual leader of the war party inside the government, was in graduate school through the late 1960s. Richard Armitage, his skeptical counterpart at the State Department and Powell's ally in pleading for restraint, is a Naval Academy graduate who served three tours in Vietnam.

I ended up thinking that the Nazi analogy paralyzes the debate about Iraq rather than clarifying it. Like any other episode in history, today's situation is both familiar and new.

In the ruthlessness of the adversary it resembles dealing with Adolf Hitler. But Iraq, unlike Germany, has no industrial base and few military allies nearby. It is split by regional, religious, and ethnic differences that are much more complicated than Nazi Germany's simple mobilization of "Aryans" against Jews. Hitler's Germany constantly expanded, but Iraq has been bottled up, by international sanctions, for more than ten years. As in the early Cold War, America faces an international ideology bent on our destruction and a country trying to develop weapons to use against us. But then we were dealing with another superpower, capable of obliterating us. Now there is a huge imbalance between the two sides in scale and power.

If we had to choose a single analogy to govern our thinking about Iraq, my candidate would be World War I. The reason is not simply the one the historian David Fromkin advanced in his book *A Peace to End All Peace:* that the division of former Ottoman Empire territories after that war created many of the enduring problems of modern Iraq and the Middle East as a whole. The Great War is also relevant as a powerful example of the limits of human imagination: specifically, imagination about the long-term consequences of war.*

The importance of imagination was stressed to me by Merrill McPeak, a retired Air Force general with misgivings

---

*If I could rewrite this "anticipatory" article with the benefit of hindsight, it would be to reemphasize this point. The central intellectual failure of the people who planned the invasion of Iraq was their inability or unwillingness to imagine where this decision might lead.

about a preemptive attack. When America entered the Vietnam War, in which McPeak flew combat missions over the jungle, the public couldn't imagine how badly combat against a "weak" foe might turn out for the United States. Since that time, and because of the Vietnam experience, we have generally overdrawn the risks of combat itself. America's small wars of the past generation, in Grenada, Haiti, and Panama, have turned out far better—tactically, at least—than many experts dared to predict. The larger ones, in the Balkans, the Persian Gulf, and Afghanistan, have as well. The "Black Hawk Down" episode in Somalia is the main exception, and it illustrates a different rule: when fighting not organized armies but stateless foes, we have underestimated our vulnerabilities.

There is an even larger realm of imagination, McPeak suggested to me. It involves the chain of events a war can set off. Wars change history in ways no one can foresee. The Egyptians who planned to attack Israel in 1967 could not imagine how profoundly what became the Six Day War would change the map and politics of the Middle East. After its lightning victory Israel seized neighboring territory, especially on the West Bank of the Jordan River, that is still at the heart of disputes with the Palestinians. Fifty years before, no one who had accurately foreseen what World War I would bring could have rationally decided to let combat begin. The war meant the collapse of three empires, the Ottoman, the Austro-Hungarian, and the Russian; the cresting of another, the British; the eventual rise of Hitler in Germany and Mussolini in Italy; and the drawing of strange new borders from the eastern Mediterranean to the Persian

Gulf, which now define the battlegrounds of the Middle East. Probably not even the United States would have found the war an attractive bargain, even though the U.S. rise to dominance began with the wounds Britain suffered in those years.

In 1990, as the United States prepared to push Iraqi troops out of Kuwait, McPeak was the Air Force chief of staff. He thought that war was necessary and advocated heavy bombing in Iraq. Now he opposes an invasion, largely because of how hard it is to imagine the full consequences of America's first purely preemptive war—and our first large war since the Spanish-American War in which we would have few or no allies.

We must use imagination on both sides of the debate: about the risks of what Saddam Hussein might do if left in place, and also about what such a war might unleash. Some members of the war party initially urged a quick in-and-out attack. Their model was the three-part formula of the "Powell doctrine": First, line up clear support—from America's political leadership, if not internationally. Then assemble enough force to leave no doubt about the outcome. Then, before the war starts, agree on how it will end and when to leave.

The in-and-out model has obviously become unrealistic. If Saddam Hussein could be destroyed by a death ray or captured by a ninja squad that sneaked into Baghdad and spirited him away, the United States might plausibly call the job done. It would still have to wonder what Iraq's next leader might do with the weapons laboratories, but the immediate problem would be solved.

Absent ninjas, getting Saddam out will mean bringing in men, machinery, and devastation. If the United States launched a big tank-borne campaign, as suggested by some of the battle plans leaked to the press, tens of thousands of soldiers, with their ponderous logistics trail, would be in the middle of a foreign country when the fighting ended. If the U.S. military relied on an air campaign against Baghdad, as other leaked plans have implied, it would inevitably kill many Iraqi civilians before it killed Saddam. One way or another, America would leave a large footprint on Iraq, which would take time to remove.

And logistics wouldn't be the only impediment to quick withdrawal. Having taken dramatic action, we would no doubt be seen—by the world and ourselves, by al-Jazeera and CNN—as responsible for the consequences. The United States could have stopped the Khmer Rouge slaughter in Cambodia in the 1970s, but it was not going to, having spent the previous decade in a doomed struggle in Vietnam. It could have prevented some of the genocide in Rwanda in the 1990s, and didn't, but at least it did not trigger the slaughter by its own actions. "It is quite possible that if we went in, took out Saddam Hussein, and then left quickly, the result would be an extremely bloody civil war," says William Galston, the director of the Institute for Philosophy and Public Policy at the University of Maryland, who was a Marine during the Vietnam War. "That blood would be directly on our hands." Most people I spoke with, whether in favor of war or not, recognized that military action is a barbed hook: once it goes in, there is no quick release.

The tone of the political debate reflects a dawning awareness of this reality. Early this year, during the strange "phony war" stage of Iraq discussions, most people in Washington assumed that war was coming, but there was little open discussion of exactly why it was necessary and what consequences it would bring. The pro-war group avoided questions about what would happen after a victory, because to consider postwar complications was to weaken the case for a preemptive strike. Some war advocates even said, if pressed, that the details of postwar life didn't matter. With the threat and the tyrant eliminated, the United States could assume that whatever regime emerged would be less dangerous than the one it replaced.

As the swirl of leaks, rumors, and official statements made an attack seem alternately more and less imminent, the increasing chaos in Afghanistan underscored a growing consensus about the in-and-out scenario for Iraq: it didn't make sense. The war itself might be quick, perhaps even quicker than the rout of the Taliban. But the end of the fighting would hardly mean the end of America's commitment. In August, as warlords reasserted their power in Afghanistan, General Tommy Franks, the U.S. commander, said that American troops might need to stay in Afghanistan for many years.

If anything, America's involvement in Afghanistan should have been cleaner and more containable than what would happen in Iraq. In Afghanistan the United States was responding to an attack, rather than initiating regime change. It had broad international support; it had the Northern Alliance to do much of the work. Because the Taliban and al-Qaeda finally chose to melt away rather than stand and fight, U.S. forces took control of the major cities while doing relatively little unintended damage. And still, getting out will take much longer than getting in.

Some proponents of war viewed the likelihood of long involvement in Iraq as a plus. If the United States went in planning to stay, it could, they contended, really make a difference there. Richard Perle addressed a major antiwar argument—that Arab states would flare up in resentment—by attempting to turn it around. "It seems at least as likely," he wrote in his *Daily Telegraph* column, "that Saddam's replacement by a decent Iraqi regime would open the way to a far more stable and peaceful region. A democratic Iraq would be a powerful refutation of the patronizing view that Arabs are incapable of democracy."*

Some regional experts made the opposite point: that a

---

*This was a relatively rare prewar appearance of what later became the administration's principal argument for the war. The importance of a liberated, democratized Iraq in transforming the entire Arab-Islamic world was always a central theme for Paul Wolfowitz and his intellectual allies. But because the perceived threat of Saddam Hussein's nuclear or biological weapons was so much more immediate and easier to grasp as a case for war, the administration spent much less time in 2002 or 2003 on subtler arguments like Perle's—important as they may have been in the administration's own decision-making.

President Bush's State of the Union speech in 2003, delivered six weeks before the beginning of combat, illustrates the point. The president's discussion of Iraq took up much of the last fifteen minutes of an hour-long speech. In the printed version of the speech, the discussion of Iraq ran for 19 paragraphs. Of those, 18 paragraphs dealt with the threat posed by

strong, prosperous, confident, stable Iraq was the last thing its neighbors, who prefer it in its bottled-up condition, wanted to see. Others pooh-poohed the notion that any Western power, however hard it tried or long it stayed, could bring about any significant change in Iraq's political culture.

Regardless of these differences, the day after a war ended, Iraq would become America's problem, for practical and political reasons. Because we would have destroyed the political order and done physical damage in the process, the claims on American resources and attention would be comparable to those of any U.S. state. Conquered Iraqis would turn to the U.S. government for emergency relief, civil order,

---

Saddam Hussein's weapons programs. For instance: "Imagine those nineteen [9/11] hijackers with other weapons and other plans—this time armed by Saddam Hussein. It would take one vial, one cannister, one crate slipped into this country to bring a day of horror like none we have ever known." And: "Some have said we must not act until the threat is imminent. Since when have terrorists and tyrants announced their intentions, politely putting us on notice before they strike? If this threat is permitted to fully and suddenly emerge, all actions, all words, and all recriminations would come too late."

The discussion of Iraq ended this way: "We will consult. But let there be no misunderstanding. If Saddam Hussein does not fully disarm, for the safety of our people and for the peace of the world, we will lead a coalition to disarm him."

The word *democracy* did not appear in the president's discussion of Iraq (though he said that America hoped to encourage democratic government among the Palestinians and in Iran). The one paragraph of his speech about internal conditions in Iraq emphasized the torture and abuse Saddam Hussein had inflicted on his own people. The speech said this, and only this, about the political future of Iraq: "And as we and our coalition partners are doing in Afghanistan, we will bring the Iraqi people food and medi-

economic reconstruction, and protection of their borders. They wouldn't be able to vote in U.S. elections, of course— although they might after they emigrated. (Every American war has created a refugee-and-immigrant stream.) But they would be part of us.

During the debate about whether to go to war, each side selectively used various postwar possibilities to bolster its case. Through the course of my interviews I found it useful to consider the possibilities as one comprehensive group. What follows is a triage list for American occupiers: the biggest problems they would face on the first day after the war, in the first week, and so on, until, perhaps decades from

---

cines and supplies—and freedom." (The text of this speech, and all other formal statements by President Bush, is available at www.whitehouse.gov.)

The same emphasis applied in Colin Powell's influential presentation to the United Nations Security Council on March 7, 2003, just before the war began. The transcript released by the U.S. government is more than 2,500 words long. Exactly one sentence in the speech was devoted to any subject other than the threat of Saddam Hussein's weapons programs and the need to disarm him. That sentence said: "As we sit here, let us not forget the horrors still going on in Iraq, with a spare moment to remember the suffering Iraqi people whose treasure is spent on these kinds of programs and not for their own benefit, people who are being brutalized and robbed by Saddam and his regime."

The speech, the last major presentation by a senior U.S. official to a world audience before combat began, said nothing whatsoever about democraticizing Iraq or setting a broader example for the Middle East.

After the war, when the evidence of supposed WMD programs had failed to appear, administration officials said they had always mentioned the political and strategic benefits of liberating Iraq—and they were right. But before the war those claims had taken a very, very distant second place to warnings about the immediate threat of Iraq's weapons.

now, they could come to grips with the long-term connections between Iraq and the United States.

THE FIRST DAY

Last-minute mayhem The biggest concern on the first day of peace would arise from what happened in the last few days of war. "I don't think that physically controlling the important parts of the country need be as difficult as many people fear," Chris Sanders, an American who worked for eighteen years in Saudi Arabia and is now a consultant in London, told me. "But of course it all depends on how one finds oneself in a victorious position—on what you had to do to win."

What would Saddam Hussein, facing defeat and perhaps death, have decided late in the war to do with the stockpiled weapons of mass destruction that were the original justification for our attack? The various Pentagon battle plans leaked to the media all assume that Iraq would use chemical weapons against U.S. troops. (Biological weapons work too slowly, and a nuclear weapon, if Iraq had one, would be more valuable for mass urban destruction than for battlefield use.) During the buildup to the Gulf War, American officials publicly warned Iraq that if it used chemical weapons against U.S. troops, we would respond with everything at our disposal, presumably including nuclear weapons. Whether or not this was a bluff, Iraq did not use chemical weapons. But if Saddam were fighting for survival, rather than for control of Kuwait, his decisions might be different.

The major chemical weapons in Iraqi arsenals are thought

to be the nerve gas sarin, also called "GB," and liquid methyl-phosphonothioic acid, or "VX."* Both can be absorbed through the lungs, the skin, or the eyes, and can cause death from amounts as small as one drop. Sarin disperses quickly, but VX is relatively nonvolatile and can pose a more lasting danger. U.S. troops would be equipped with protective suits, but these are cumbersome and retain heat; the need to wear them has been an argument for delaying an attack until winter.

Another concern is that on his way down Saddam would use chemical weapons not only tactically, to slow or kill attacking U.S. soldiers, but also strategically, to lash out beyond his borders. In particular, he could use them against Israel. Iraq's SCUD and "al-Hussein" missiles cannot reach Europe or North America. But Israel is in easy range—as Iraq demonstrated during the Gulf War, when it launched forty-two SCUDs against Israel. (It also launched more than forty against the allied troops; all these SCUDs had conventional explosive warheads, rather than chemical payloads.) During the Gulf War the Israeli government of Yitzhak Shamir complied with urgent U.S. requests that it leave all retaliation to the Americans, rather than broadening the

---

*After the war was over, American officials realized that they hadn't needed to worry about sarin, VX, or other gruesome retaliatory possibilities. Saddam Hussein did not have these weapons. Moreover, according to an account published in *Foreign Affairs* in 2006, he was so deluded about the military realities of his situation that he failed to believe the United States would actually attack. Therefore he failed to take even minimal defensive steps like blowing up bridges to slow the U.S. drive toward Baghdad. Because U.S. military planners could not have known or assumed this level of incompetence on Saddam Hussein's part, they had no choice but to suit up their troops with heavy, cumbersome protective gear.

war by launching its own attacks. Nothing in Ariel Sharon's long career suggests that he could be similarly restrained.

A U.S. occupation of Iraq, then, could begin with the rest of the Middle East at war around it. "What's the worst nightmare at the start?" a retired officer who fought in the Gulf War asked me rhetorically. "Saddam Hussein hits Israel, and Sharon hits some Arab city, maybe in Saudi Arabia. Then you have the all-out religious war that the Islamic fundamentalists and maybe some Likudniks are itching for."

This is more a worst-case prediction than a probability, so let's assume that any regional combat could be contained and that we would get relatively quickly to the challenges of the following, postwar days.

THE FIRST WEEK

Refugees and relief However quick and surgical the battle might seem to the American public, however much brighter Iraq's long-term prospects might become, in the short term many Iraqis would be desperate. Civilians would have been killed, to say nothing of soldiers. Bodies would need to be buried, wounds dressed, orphans located and cared for, hospitals staffed.

"You are going to start right out with a humanitarian crisis," says William Nash, of the Council on Foreign Relations.*

---

*Most military and civilian officials with experience in past occupations or postwar scenarios shared this assumption. When they all proved to be wrong, and no mass refugee flows followed the fighting, officials of the

A retired two-star army general, Nash was in charge of postcombat relief operations in southern Iraq after the Gulf War and later served in Bosnia and Kosovo. Most examples in this article, from Nash and others, involve the occupation of Kuwait and parts of Iraq after the Gulf War, rather than ongoing operations in Afghanistan. The campaign in Afghanistan may have a rhetorical connection to a future war in Iraq, in that both are part of the general "war on terror"; but otherwise the circumstances are very different. Iraq and Afghanistan are unlike in scale, geography, history, and politics, not to mention in the U.S. objectives and military plans that relate to them. And enough time has passed to judge the effects of the Gulf War, which is not true of Afghanistan.

"In the drive to Baghdad, you are going to do a lot of damage," Nash told me. "Either you will destroy a great deal of infrastructure by trying to isolate the battlefield—or they will destroy it, trying to delay your advance."* Postwar

Bush administration claimed that it was hypocritical of anyone to complain about the Administration's own failures of foresight about postwar Iraq. After all, no one had the faintest idea what was going to occur!

That rebuttal is not convincing. The main reason there was no refugee crisis was that Saddam Hussein had no secret stores of chemical, biological, or nuclear weapons. The prewar scenarios that envisioned millions of displaced Iraqis assumed that people would be fleeing cities devastated by Saddam in a retaliatory strike. All the other main themes of the prewar planning mentioned in this book—the importance of maintaining public order, the likely resentment of an occupying force, the importance of regional and ethnic friction—turned out to be prescient.

*Nash proved to be right about the importance of preserving the country's infrastructure, and the risks of letting it be damaged. He failed to foresee the major source of destruction: not the fighting itself in March and April of 2003 but the uncontrolled looting of the following two months.

commerce and recovery in Iraq will depend, of course, on roads, the rail system, airfields, and bridges across the Tigris and the Euphrates—facilities that both sides in the war will have incentives to blow up. "So you've got to find the village elders," Nash continued, "and say, 'Let's get things going. Where are the wells? I can bring you food, but bringing you enough water is really hard.' Right away you need food, water, and shelter—these people have to survive. Because you started the war, you have accepted a moral responsibility for them. And you may well have totally obliterated the social and political structure that had been providing these services."

Most of the military and diplomatic figures I interviewed stressed the same thing. In August, Scott Feil, a retired army colonel who now directs a study project for the Association of the United States Army on postwar reconstruction, said at a Senate hearing, "I think the international community will hold the United States primarily responsible for the outcome in the postconflict reconstruction effort." Charles William Maynes, a former editor of *Foreign Policy* magazine and now the president of the Eurasia Foundation, told me, "Because of the allegations that we've been killing women and children over the years with the sanctions, we are going to be all the more responsible for restoring the infrastructure."

This is not impossible, but it is expensive. Starting in the first week, whoever is in charge in Iraq would need food, tents, portable hospitals, water-purification systems, generators, and so on. During the Clinton administration, Frederick Barton directed the Office of Transition Initiatives at the United States Agency for International Development (USAID), which worked with State and Defense Department representatives on postwar recovery efforts in countries such as Haiti, Liberia, and Bosnia. He told me, "These places typically have no revenue systems, no public funds, no way anybody at any level of governance can do anything right away. You've got to pump money into the system." Exactly how much is hard to say. Scott Feil has estimated that costs for the first year in Iraq would be about $16 billion for postconflict security forces and $1 billion for reconstruction—presumably all from the United States, because of the lack of allies in the war.

Catching Saddam Hussein While the refugees were being attended to, an embarrassing leftover problem might persist. From the U.S. perspective, it wouldn't really matter whether the war left Saddam dead, captured, or in exile. What would matter is that his whereabouts were known. The only outcome nearly as bad as leaving him in power would be having him at large, like Osama bin Laden and much of the al-Qaeda leadership in the months after the September 11 attacks.

"My nightmare scenario," Merrill McPeak, the former air force chief of staff, told me, "is that we jump people in, seize the airport, bring in the 101st [Airborne Division]— and we can't find Saddam Hussein. Then we've got Osama and Saddam Hussein out there, both of them achieving mythical heroic status in the Arab world just by surviving.

It's not a trivial problem to actually grab the guy, and it ain't over until you've got him in handcuffs."

During the Gulf War, McPeak and his fellow commanders learned that Saddam was using a fleet of Winnebago-like vehicles to move around Baghdad. They tried to track the vehicles but never located Saddam himself. As McPeak concluded from reading psychological profiles of the Iraqi dictator, he is not only a thug and a murderer but an extremely clever adversary. "My concern is that he is smarter individually than our bureaucracy is collectively," he told me. "Bureaucracies tend to dumb things down. So in trying to find him, we have a chess match between a bureaucracy and Saddam Hussein."

THE FIRST MONTH

Police control, manpower, and intelligence When the lid comes off after a long period of repression, people may be grateful and elated. But they may also be furious and vengeful, as the postliberation histories of Romania and Kosovo indicate. Phebe Marr, a veteran Iraq expert who until her retirement taught at the National Defense University, told a Senate committee in August,* "If firm leadership is not in place in Baghdad the day after Saddam is removed, retribu-

---

*The hearings occurred as this article was going to press. We delayed the article's close until the hearings were completed. An early version of the article was posted on the *Atlantic*'s Web site three weeks after the hearings.

tion, score settling, and bloodletting, especially in urban areas, could take place." William Nash, who supervised Iraqi prisoners in liberated parts of Kuwait, told me, "The victim becomes the aggressor. You try to control it, but you'll just find the bodies in the morning."

Some policing of conquered areas, to minimize warlordism and freelance justice, is an essential step toward making the postwar era seem like an occupation rather than simple chaos. Doing it right requires enough people to do the policing; a reliable way to understand local feuds and tensions; and a plan for creating and passing power to a local constabulary. Each can be more complicated than it sounds.

Simply manning a full occupation force would be a challenge. In the occupation business there are some surprising rules of thumb. Whether a country is big or small, for instance, the surrender of weapons by the defeated troops seems to take about 120 days. Similarly, regardless of a country's size, maintaining order seems to take about one occupation soldier or police officer for each 500 people—plus one supervisor for each ten policemen. For Iraq's 23 million people that would mean an occupation force of about 50,000. Scott Feil told a Senate committee that he thought the occupation would need 75,000 security soldiers.

In most of its military engagements since Vietnam the United States has enthusiastically passed many occupation duties to allied or United Nations forces. Ideally the designated occupiers of Iraq would be other Arabs—similar rather than alien to most Iraqis in language, religion, and ethnicity. But persuading other countries to clean up after a war they had opposed would be quite a trick.

Providing even 25,000 occupiers on a sustained basis would not be easy for the U.S. military.* Over the past decade the military's head count has gone down, even as its level of foreign commitment and the defense budget have gone up. All the active-duty forces together total about 1.4 million people. Five years ago it was about 1.5 million. At the time of the Gulf War the total was over two million. With fewer people available, the military's "ops tempo" (essentially, the level of overtime) has risen, dramatically in the past year. Since the terrorist attacks some 40,000 soldiers who had planned to retire or leave the service have been obliged to stay, under "stop-loss" personnel policies. In July the army awarded a $205 million contract to ITT Federal Services to provide "rent-a-cop" security guards for U.S. bases in Bosnia, sparing soldiers the need to stand guard duty. As of the beginning of September, the number of National Guard and Reserves soldiers mobilized by federal call-ups was about 80,000, compared with about 5,600 just before September 11, 2001. For the country in general the war in Central Asia has been largely a spectator event—no war bonds, no gasoline taxes, no mandatory public service. For the volunteer military on both active and reserve duty it has been quite real.

---

*The U.S. military's ability to withstand a long and large-scale deployment in Iraq got little attention before the war, no doubt because so few people imagined that more than 100,000 troops would still be there three years after the fall of Baghdad. But from the military's perspective, the difficulty of maintaining the presence was becoming a truly major challenge within a year of the invasion. This topic comes up again on pages 140–141 of this book.

One way to put more soldiers in Iraq would be to redeploy them from overseas bases. Before the attacks about 250,000 soldiers were based outside U.S. borders, more than half of them in Germany, Japan, and Korea. The American military now stations more than 118,000 soldiers in Europe alone.

But in the short term the occupation would need people from the civil-affairs specialties of the military: people trained in setting up courts and police systems, restoring infrastructure, and generally leading a war-recovery effort. Many are found in the Reserves, and many have already been deployed to missions in Bosnia, Kosovo, or elsewhere. "These are an odd bunch of people," James Dunnigan, the editor of Strategypage.com, told me. "They tend to be civilians who are overeducated—they like working for the government and having adventures at the same time. They're like the characters in *Three Kings*, without finding the gold."

One of the people Dunnigan was referring to specifically is Evan Brooks. In his normal life Brooks is an attorney at Internal Revenue Service headquarters. He is also an amateur military historian, and until his recent retirement was a lieutenant colonel in the Army Reserves, specializing in civil affairs. "Between 1947 and 1983," Brooks told me, "the number of civil-affairs units that were activated [from the Reserves] could be counted on one hand. Since 1987 there has not been a single Christmas where the DC–area civil-affairs unit has not had people deployed overseas." Brooks was the military interface with the Kuwaiti Red Crescent for several months after the Gulf War; though he is Jewish, he became a popular figure among his Muslim colleagues, and was the only American who attended Kuwaiti subcabinet meetings. "My ambition was to be military governor of Basra [the Iraqi region closest to Kuwait]," he told me, I think whimsically. "I never quite achieved it."

Wherever the occupying force finds its manpower, it will face the challenge of understanding politics and rivalries in a country whose language few Americans speak. The CIA and the Army Special Forces have been recruiting Arabic speakers and grilling Iraqi exiles for local intelligence. The Pentagon's leadership includes at least one Arabic speaker: the director of the Joint Staff, John Abizaid, a three-star general. As a combat commander during the Gulf War, Abizaid was able to speak directly with Iraqis. Most American occupiers will lack this skill.

Inability to communicate could be disastrous. After the Gulf War, William Nash told me, he supervised camps containing Iraqi refugees and captured members of the Republican Guard. "We had a couple of near riots—mini-riots—in the refugee camps when Saddam's agents were believed to have infiltrated," Nash said. "We brought a guy in, and a group of refugees in the camp went berserk. Somebody said, 'He's an agent!' My guys had to stop them or they were going to tear the man to shreds. We put a bag over his head and hustled him out of there, just to save his life. And when that happens, you have no idea what kind of vendetta you've just fallen in the middle of. You have no idea if it's a six-camel issue or something much more. I take that experience from 1991 and square it fifty times for a larger country. That would be a postwar Iraq."

Eventually the occupiers would solve the problem by fostering a local police force, as part of a new Iraqi government. "You have to start working toward local, civilian-led police," Frederick Barton, the former USAID official, told me. "Setting up an academy is okay, but national police forces tend to be sources of future coups and corruption. I'd rather have a hundred and fifty small forces around the country and take my chances on thirty of them being corrupt than have a centralized force and end up with one big, bad operation."

Forming a government Tyrants make a point of crushing any challenge to their power. When a tyranny falls, therefore, a new, legitimate source of authority may take time to emerge. If potential new leaders are easy to identify, it is usually because of their family name or record of political struggle. Corazón Aquino illustrates the first possibility: as the widow of a political rival whom Ferdinand Marcos had ordered killed, she was the ideal successor to Marcos in the Philippines (despite her later troubles in office). Charles de Gaulle in postwar France, Nelson Mandela in South Africa, and Kim Dae-jung in South Korea illustrate the second. Should the Burmese military ever fall, Aung San Suu Kyi will have both qualifications for leadership.

Iraq has no such obvious sources of new leadership. A word about its political history is useful in explaining the succession problem. From the 1500s onward the Ottoman Empire, based in Istanbul, controlled the territory that is now Iraq. When the empire fell, after World War I, Great

Britain assumed supervision of the newly created Kingdom of Iraq, under a mandate from the League of Nations. The British imported a member of Syria's Hashemite royal family, who in 1921 became King Faisal I of Iraq. (The Hashemites, one of whom is still on the throne in Jordan, claim descent not only from the prophet Muhammad but also from the Old Testament Abraham.) The Kingdom of Iraq lasted until 1958, when King Faisal II was overthrown and killed in a military coup. In 1963 the Baath, or "renewal," party took power in another coup—which the United States initially welcomed, in hopes that the Baathists would be anticommunist. By the late 1970s Saddam Hussein had risen to dominance within the party.

The former monarchy is too shallow-rooted to survive reintroduction to Iraq, and Saddam has had time to eliminate nearly all sources of internal resistance. The Kurdish chieftains of the northern provinces are the primary exception. But their main impulse has been separatist: they seek autonomy from the government in Baghdad and feud with one another. That leaves Iraqi exile groups—especially the Iraqi National Congress (INC)—as the likeliest suppliers of leaders.

The INC survives on money from the U.S. government. The organization and its president, a U.S.-trained businessman named Ahmad Chalabi, have sincere supporters and also detractors within the Washington policy world. The columnist Jim Hoagland, of *The Washington Post,* has called Chalabi a "dedicated advocate of democracy" who has "sacrifice[d] most of his fortune so he can risk his life to fight Saddam." The case against Chalabi involves his fortune too: he is a high-living character, and under him the INC has been dogged by accusations of financial mismanagement. "The opposition outside Iraq is almost as divided, weak, and irrelevant as the White Russians in the 1920s," says Anthony Cordesman, of the Center for Strategic and International Studies (CSIS), in Washington.

"What you will need is a man with a black moustache," a retired British spy who once worked in the region told me. "Out of chaos I am sure someone will emerge. But it can't be Chalabi, and it probably won't be a democracy. Democracy is a strange fruit, and, cynically, to hold it together in the short term you need a strongman."

Several U.S. soldiers told me that the comfortable Powell doctrine, with its emphasis on swift action and a clear exit strategy, could make the inevitable difficulty and delay in setting up plausible new leadership even more frustrating.

When British administrators supervised the former Ottoman lands in the 1920s, they liked to insinuate themselves into the local culture, à la Lawrence of Arabia. "Typically, a young man would go there in his twenties, would master the local dialects, would have a local mistress before he settled down to something more respectable," Victor O'Reilly, an Irish novelist who specializes in military topics, told me. "They were to achieve tremendous amounts with minimal resources. They ran huge chunks of the world this way, and it was psychological. They were hugely knowledgeable and got deeply involved with the locals." The original Green Berets tried to use a version of this approach in Vietnam, and to an extent it is still the ideal for the Special Forces.

But in the generation since Vietnam the mainstream U.S.

military has gone in the opposite direction: toward a definition of its role in strictly martial terms. It is commonplace
these days in discussions with officers to hear them describe
their mission as "killing people and blowing things up." The
phrase is used deliberately to shock civilians, and also for its
absolute clarity as to what a "military response" involves. If
this point is understood, there can be no confusion about
what the military is supposed to do when a war starts, no recriminations when it uses all necessary force, and as little
risk as possible that soldiers will die "political" deaths because they've been constrained for symbolic or diplomatic
reasons from fully defending themselves. All this is in keeping with the more familiar parts of the Powell doctrine—the
insistence on political backing and overwhelming force. The
goal is to protect the U.S. military from being misused.

The strict segregation of military and political functions
may be awkward in Iraq, however. In the short term the U.S.
military would necessarily be the government of Iraq. In the
absence of international allies or UN support, and the absence of an obvious Iraqi successor regime, American soldiers would have to make and administer political decisions
on the fly. America's two most successful occupations embraced the idea that military officials must play political
roles. Emperor Hirohito remained the titular head of state
in occupied Japan, but Douglas MacArthur, a lifelong soldier, was immersed in the detailed reconstruction of Japan's
domestic order. In occupied Germany, General Lucius D.
Clay did something comparable, though less flamboyantly.
Today's Joint Chiefs of Staff would try to veto any suggestion for a MacArthur-like proconsul. U.S. military leaders in

the Balkans have pushed this role onto the United Nations. Exactly who could assume it in Iraq is not clear.

In the first month, therefore, the occupiers would face a paradox: the institution best equipped to exercise power as a local government—the U.S. military—would be the one most reluctant to do so.

Territorial integrity This is where the exercise of power might first be put to a major test. In ancient times what is now central Iraq was the cradle of civilization, Mesopotamia ("Mespot" in Fleet Street shorthand during the British-mandate era). Under the Ottoman Empire today's Iraq was not one province but three, and the divisions still affect current politics. The province of Baghdad, in the center of the country, is the stronghold of Iraq's Sunni Muslim minority. Sunnis dominated administrative positions in the Ottoman days and have controlled the army and the government ever since, even though they make up only about 20 percent of the population. The former province of Mosul, in the mountainous north, is the stronghold of Kurdish tribes, which make up 15 to 20 percent of the population. Through the years they have both warred against and sought common cause with other Kurdish tribes across Iraq's borders in Turkey, Iran, and Syria. Mosul also has some of the country's richest reserves of oil. The former province of Basra, to the southeast, borders Iran, Kuwait, and the Persian Gulf. Its population is mainly Shiite Muslims, who make up the majority in the country as a whole but have little political power.

The result of this patchwork is a country like Indonesia

or Soviet-era Yugoslavia. Geographic, ethnic, and religious forces tend to pull it apart; only an offsetting pull from a strong central government keeps it in one piece. Most people think that under the stress of regime change Iraq would be more like Indonesia after Suharto than like Yugoslavia after Tito—troubled but intact. But the strains will be real.

"In my view it is very unlikely—indeed, inconceivable—that Iraq will break up into three relatively cohesive components," Phebe Marr, the Iraq expert, told the Senate Committee on Foreign Relations. But a weakened center could mean all sorts of problems, she said, even if the country were officially whole. The Kurds could seize the northern oil fields, for example. The Turkish government has long made clear that if Iraq cannot control its Kurdish population, Turkey—concerned about separatist movements in its own Kurdish provinces—will step in to do the job. "Turkey could intervene in the north, as it has done before," Marr said. "Iran, through its proxies, could follow suit. There could even be a reverse flow of refugees as many Iraqi Shia exiles in Iran return home, possibly in the thousands, destabilizing areas in the south."

The centrifugal forces acting on postwar Iraq, even if they did not actually break up the country, would present a situation different from those surrounding past U.S. occupations. America's longest experience as an occupier was in the Philippines, which the United States controlled formally or informally for most of a century. Many ethnic, linguistic, and religious differences separated the people of the Philippine archipelago, but because the islands have no land frontier with another country, domestic tensions could be managed with few international complications. And in dealing with Japan and Germany after World War II, the United States wanted, if anything, to dilute each country's sense of distinct national identity. There was also no doubt about the boundaries of those occupied countries.

Postwar Iraq, in contrast, would have less-than-certain boundaries, internal tensions with international implications, and highly nervous neighbors. Six countries share borders with Iraq. Clockwise from the Persian Gulf, they are Kuwait, Saudi Arabia, Jordan, Syria, Turkey, and Iran. None of them has wanted Saddam to expand Iraq's territory. But they would be oddly threatened by a post-Saddam breakup or implosion. The Turks, as noted, have a particular interest in preventing any country's Kurdish minority from rebelling or forming a separatist state. The monarchies of Saudi Arabia and Jordan fear that riots and chaos in Iraq could provoke similar upheaval among their own peoples.

"In states like the United Arab Emirates and Qatar, even Saudi Arabia," says Shibley Telhami, the Anwar Sadat Professor of Peace and Development at the University of Maryland, "there is the fear that the complete demise of Iraq would in the long run play into the hands of Iran, which they see as even more of a threat." Iran is four times as large as Iraq, and has nearly three times as many people. Although it is Islamic, its population and heritage are Persian, not Arab; to the Arab states, Iran is "them," not "us."

As Arab regimes in the region assess the possible outcomes

29

of a war, Telhami says, "they see instability, at a minimum, for a long period of time, and in the worst case the disintegration of the Iraqi state." These fears matter to the United States, because of oil. Chaos in the Persian Gulf would disrupt world oil markets and therefore the world economy. Significant expansion of Iran's influence, too, would work against the Western goal of balancing regional power among Saudi Arabia, Iran, and postwar Iraq. So as the dust of war cleared, keeping Iraq together would suddenly be America's problem. If the Kurds rebelled in the north, if the Shiite government in Iran tried to "reclaim" the southern districts of Iraq in which fellow Shiites live, the occupation powers would have to respond—even by sending in U.S. troops for follow-up battles.

THE FIRST YEAR

"Denazification" and "loya-jirgazation" As the months pass, an occupation force should, according to former occupiers, spend less time reacting to crises and more time undertaking long-term projects such as improving schools, hospitals, and housing. Iraq's occupiers would meanwhile also have to launch their version of "denazification": identifying and punishing those who were personally responsible for the old regime's brutality, without launching a Khmer Rouge–style purge of everyone associated with the former government.*

---

*As it turned out, the counterpart of "denazification" became a major point of controversy, and a major apparent failure, in the U.S. occupation

Depending on what happened to Saddam and his closest associates, war-crime trials might begin. Even if the United States had carried out the original invasion on its own, the occupiers would seek international support for these postwar measures.

In the early months the occupiers would also begin an Iraqi version of "loya-jirgazation"—that is, supporting a "grand council" or convention like the one at which the Afghans selected the leadership for their transitional government. Here the occupation would face a fundamental decision about its goals within Iraq.

One option was described to me by an American diplomat as the "decent interval" strategy. The United States would help to set up the framework for a new governing system and then transfer authority to it as soon as possible—whether or not the new regime was truly ready to exercise control. This is more or less the approach the United States and its allies have taken in Afghanistan: once the *loya jirga* had set up an interim government and Hamid Karzai was in place as president, the United States was happy to act as if this were a true government. The situation in Afghanistan

---

of Iraq. The original occupation plans called for peeling off a relatively shallow layer of former senior officials in the Iraqi military, and then reconstituting most rank-and-file soldiers into a new Iraqi force. But as described on pages 102–104 and 158–161 of this book, on his arrival as head of the Coalition Provisional Authority, Paul "Jerry" Bremer changed this policy and ordered a sweeping dissolution of the entire preexisting Iraqi army. By most accounts this decision, and the counterpart policy of sweeping "de-Baathification," were major mistakes that set back the effort to restore order in Iraq.

shows the contradictions in this strategy. It works only if the United States decides it doesn't care about the Potemkin government's lapses and limitations—for instance, an inability to suppress warlords and ethnic-regional feuds. In Afghanistan the United States still does care, so there is growing tension between the pretense of Afghan sovereignty and the reality of U.S. influence. However complicated the situation in Afghanistan is proving to be, things are, again, likely to be worse in Iraq. The reasons are familiar: a large local army, the Northern Alliance, had played a major role in the fight against the Taliban; a natural leader, Karzai, was available; the invasion itself had been a quasi-international rather than a U.S.-only affair.

The other main option would be something closer to U.S. policy in occupied Japan: a slow, thorough effort to change fundamental social and cultural values, in preparation for a sustainable democracy. Japan's version of democracy departs from the standard Western model in various ways, but a system even half as open and liberal as Japan's would be a huge step for Iraq. The transformation of Japan was slow. It required detailed interference in the day-to-day workings of Japanese life. U.S. occupation officials supervised what was taught in Japanese classrooms. Douglas MacArthur's assistants not only rewrote the labor laws but wrote the constitution itself. They broke up big estates and reallocated the land. Carrying out this transformation required an effort comparable to the New Deal. American lawyers, economists, engineers, and administrators by the thousands spent years developing and executing reform plans. Transformation did not happen by fiat. It won't in Iraq either.

John Dower, a professor of history at MIT, is a leading historian of the U.S. occupation of Japan; his book *Embracing Defeat* won the Pulitzer Prize for nonfiction in 2000. Dower points out that in Japan occupation officials had a huge advantage they presumably would not have in Iraq: no one questioned their legitimacy. The victorious Americans had not only the power to impose their will on Japan but also, in the world's eyes, the undoubted right to remake a militarist society. "Every country in Asia wanted this to be done," Dower says. "Every country in the world." The same was true in postwar Germany. The absence of international support today is one of many reasons Dower vehemently opposes a preemptive attack.

Oil and money Iraq could be the Saudi Arabia of the future. Partly because its output has been constrained by ten years' worth of sanctions, and mainly because it has never embraced the international oil industry as Saudi Arabia has, it is thought to have some of the largest untapped reserves in the world. Saudi Arabia now exports much more oil than Iraq—some seven million barrels a day versus about two million. But Iraq's output could rapidly increase.

The supply-demand balance in the world's energy markets is expected to shift over the next five years. Import demand continues to rise—even more quickly in China and India than in the United States. Production in most of the world is flat or declining—in OPEC-producing countries, by OPEC fiat. The role of Persian Gulf suppliers will only become more important; having two large suppliers in the Gulf rather than just one will be a plus for consumers. So in the Arab world the U.S. crusade against Saddam looks to be motivated less by fears of terrorism and weapons of mass destruction than by the wish to defend Israel and the desire for oil.

Ideally, Iraq's reentry into the world oil market would be smooth. Production would be ramped up quickly enough to generate money to rebuild the Iraqi economy and infrastructure, but gradually enough to keep Saudi Arabia from feeling threatened and retaliating in ways that could upset the market. International oil companies, rather than an occupation authority, would do most of the work here. What would the occupiers need to think about? First, the threat of sabotage, which would become greater to the extent that Iraq's oil industry was seen in the Arab world more as a convenience for Western consumers than as a source of wealth for Iraq. Since many of the wells are in the Kurdish regions, Kurdish rebellion or dissatisfaction could put them at risk. Oil pipelines, seemingly so exposed, are in fact not the likeliest target. "Pipes are always breaking, so we know how to fix them quickly," says Peter Schwartz, of the Global Business Network, who worked for years as an adviser to Shell Oil. At greatest risk are the terminals at seaports, where oil is loaded into tankers, and the wells themselves. At the end of the Gulf War, Iraqi troops set fire to 90 percent of Kuwait's wells, which burned for months. Wellheads and terminals are the sites that oil companies protect most carefully.*

---

*The Brookings Institution's "Iraq Index," available online at http://www.brookings.edu/fp/saban/iraq/index.pdf, has tracked social, economic, and political indicators in Iraq month by month since the invasion. Ac-

Another challenge to recovery prospects in general would be Iraq's amazingly heavy burden of debt. Iraq was directed by the United Nations to pay reparations for the damage it inflicted on Kuwait during the Gulf War. That and other debts have compounded to amounts the country cannot hope to repay. Estimates vary, but the range—$200 billion to $400 billion—illustrates the problem.

"Leaving Iraq saddled with a massive debt and wartime-reparations bill because of Saddam is an act of moral and ethical cowardice," says Anthony Cordesman, of the Center for Strategic and International Studies, a military expert who is no one's idea of a bleeding heart. "We must show the Arab and Islamic worlds that we will not profiteer in any way from our victory. We must persuade the world to forgive past debts and reparations." Cordesman and others argue that as part of regime change the United States would have to take responsibility for solving this problem. Otherwise Iraq would be left in the position of Weimar Germany after the Treaty of Versailles: crushed by unpayable reparations.

This would be only part of the financial reality of regime change. The overall cost of U.S. military operations during the Gulf War came to some $61 billion. Because of the contributions it received from Japan, Saudi Arabia, and other

---

cording to this index, before the war Iraq was producing roughly 2.5 million barrels of crude oil per day. The output fell immediately after the war and then recovered very slowly. By March 2006, total crude oil production was only 80 percent of its prewar level, or about 2 million barrels per day.

countries in its alliance, the United States wound up in the convenient yet embarrassing position of having most of that cost reimbursed. An assault on Iraq would be at least as expensive and would all be on our tab. Add to that the price of recovery aid. It is hard to know even how to estimate the total cost.

Legitimacy and unilateralism An important premise for the American war party is that squawks and hand-wringing from Arab governments cannot be taken seriously. The Saudis may say they oppose an attack; the Jordanians may publicly warn against it; but in fact most governments in the region would actually be glad to have the Saddam wild card removed. And if some countries didn't welcome the outcome, all would adjust to the reality of superior U.S. force once the invasion was a fait accompli. As for the Europeans, they are thought to have a poor record in threat assessment. Unlike the United States, Europe has not really been responsible since World War II for life-and-death judgments about military problems, and Europeans tend to whine and complain. American war advocates say that Europe's reluctance to confront Saddam is like its reluctance to recognize the Soviet threat a generation ago. Europeans thought Ronald Reagan was a brute for calling the Soviet Union an "evil empire." According to this view, they are just as wrongheaded to consider George W. Bush a simpleton for talking today about an "axis of evil."

Still, support from the rest of the world can be surprisingly comforting. Most Americans were moved by the outpouring of solidarity on September 11—the flowers in front of embassies, the astonishing headline in *Le Monde:* "NOUS SOMMES TOUS AMÉRICAINS." By the same token, foreigners' hatred can be surprisingly demoralizing. Think of the news clips of exaltation in Palestinian camps after the attacks, or the tape of Osama bin Laden chortling about how many people he had killed. The United States rarely turned to the United Nations from the late 1960s through the mid-1980s, because the UN was so often a forum for anti-American rants. Resentment against America in the Arab world has led to a partial boycott of U.S. exports, which so far has not mattered much. It has also fueled the recruitment of suicide terrorists, which has mattered a great deal.

The presence or absence of allies would have both immediate and long-term consequences for the occupation. No matter how welcome as liberators they may be at first, foreign soldiers eventually wear out their welcome. It would be far easier if this inescapably irritating presence were varied in nationality, under a UN flag, rather than all American. All the better if the force were Islamic and Arabic-speaking.

The face of the occupying force will matter not just in Iraq's cities but also on its borders. Whoever controls Iraq will need to station forces along its most vulnerable frontier—the long flank with Iran, where at least half a million soldiers died during the 1980–88 Iran–Iraq War. The Iranians will notice any U.S. presence on the border. "As the occupying power, we will be responsible for the territorial integrity of the Iraqi state," says Charles William Maynes, of the Eurasia Foundation. "That means we will have to move our troops to the border with Iran. At that point Iran becomes our permanent enemy." *

The longer-term consequences would flow from having undertaken a war that every country in the region except Israel officially opposed. Chris Sanders, the consultant who used to work in Saudi Arabia, says that unless the United States can drum up some Arab allies, an attack on Iraq "will accomplish what otherwise would have been impossible—a bloc of regional opposition that transcends the very real differences of interests and opinions that had kept a unified Arab bloc from arising." Sanders adds dryly, "If I were an American strategic thinker, I would imagine that not to be in my interest."

THE LONG RUN

So far we've considered the downside—which, to be fair, is most of what I heard in my interviews. But there was also a distinctly positive theme, and it came from some of the most dedicated members of the war party. Their claim, again, was

---

*As it happened, the United States placed relatively few of its troops along Iraq's border with Iran. At first this was because British troops were responsible for much of that southeastern part of Iraq after the invasion. Later, as insurgent activity intensified in the center and west of the country, U.S. forces naturally concentrated there. As the United States moved toward a showdown with Iran over Iran's plans to build a nuclear weapon, Iran's growing political and religious influence in the Shiite regions of Iraq gave Iran greater leverage over America—as described in the final chapter of this book.

that forcing regime change would not just have a negative virtue—that of removing a threat. It would also create the possibility of bringing to Iraq, and eventually the whole Arab world, something it has never known before: stable democracy in an open-market system.

"This could be a golden opportunity to begin to change the face of the Arab world," James Woolsey, a former CIA director who is one of the most visible advocates of war, told me. "Just as what we did in Germany changed the face of Central and Eastern Europe, here we have got a golden chance." In this view, the fall of the Soviet empire really did mark what Francis Fukuyama called "the end of history": the democratic-capitalist model showed its superiority over other social systems. The model has many local variations; it brings adjustment problems; and it encounters resistance, such as the antiglobalization protests of the late 1990s. But it spreads—through the old Soviet territory, through Latin America and Asia, nearly everywhere except through tragic Africa and the Islamic-Arab lands of the Middle East. To think that Arab states don't want a democratic future is dehumanizing. To think they're incapable of it is worse. What is required is a first Arab democracy, and Iraq can be the place.

"If you only look forward, you can see how hard it would be to do," Woolsey said. "Everybody can say, 'Oh, sure, you're going to democratize the Middle East.'" Indeed, that was the reaction of most of the diplomats, spies, and soldiers I spoke with—"the ruminations of insane people," one British official said.

Woolsey continued with his point: "But if you look at

what we and our allies have done with the three world wars of the twentieth century—two hot, one cold—and what we've done in the interstices, we've already achieved this for two-thirds of the world. Eighty-five years ago, when we went into World War I, there were eight or ten democracies at the time. Now it's around a hundred and twenty—some free, some partly free. An order of magnitude! The compromises we made along the way, whether allying with Stalin or Franco or Pinochet, we have gotten around to fixing, and their successor regimes are democracies.

"Around half of the states of sub-Saharan Africa are democratic. Half of the twenty-plus non-Arab Muslim states. We have all of Europe except Belarus and occasionally parts of the Balkans. If you look back at what has happened in less than a century, then getting the Arab world plus Iran moving in the same direction looks a lot less awesome. It's not Americanizing the world. It's Athenizing it. And it is doable."

Richard Perle, Secretary of Defense Donald Rumsfeld, and others have presented similar prospects. Thomas McInerney, a retired three-star general, said at the Senate hearings this past summer, "Our longer-term objectives will be to bring a democratic government to Iraq . . . that will influence the region significantly." At a Pentagon briefing a few days later Rumsfeld asked rhetorically, "Wouldn't it be a wonderful thing if Iraq were similar to Afghanistan—if a bad regime was thrown out, people were liberated, food could come in, borders could be opened, repression could stop, prisons could be opened? I mean, it would be fabulous."

The transforming vision is not, to put it mildly, the consensus among those with long experience in the Middle East. "It is so divorced from any historical context, just so far out of court, that it is laughable," Chris Sanders told me. "There isn't a society in Iraq to turn into a democracy. That doesn't mean you can't set up institutions and put stooges in them. But it would make about as much sense as the South Vietnamese experiment did." Others made similar points.

Woolsey and his allies might be criticized for lacking a tragic imagination about where war might lead, but at least they recognize that it will lead somewhere. If they are more optimistic in their conclusions than most of the other people I spoke with, they do see that America's involvement in Iraq would be intimate and would be long.

It has become a cliché in popular writing about the natural world that small disturbances to complex systems can have unpredictably large effects. The world of nations is perhaps not quite as intricate as the natural world, but it certainly holds the potential for great surprise. Merely itemizing the foreseeable effects of a war with Iraq suggests reverberations that would be felt for decades. If we can judge from past wars, the effects we can't imagine when the fighting begins will prove to be the ones that matter most.

BLIND INTO BAGHDAD

JANUARY 2004

On a Friday afternoon in November 2003, I met Douglas Feith in his office at the Pentagon to discuss what has happened in Iraq. Feith's title is undersecretary of defense for policy, which places him, along with several other undersecretaries, just below Secretary of Defense Donald Rumsfeld and Deputy Secretary Paul Wolfowitz in the Pentagon's hierarchy. Informally he is seen in Washington as "Wolfowitz's Wolfowitz"—that is, as a deputy who has a wide range of responsibilities but is clearly identified with one particular policy. That policy is bringing regime change to Iraq—a goal that both Wolfowitz and Feith strongly advocated through the 1990s. To opponents of the war in Iraq, Feith is one of several shadowy, Rasputinlike figures who are shaping U.S. policy. He is seen much the way enemies of the Clinton administration saw Hillary Clinton. Others associated with the Bush administration who are seen this way include the consultant Richard Perle; Lewis "Scooter" Libby, the chief of staff for Vice President Dick Cheney; and the vice president himself. What these officials have in common is their presumably great private influence and—even in the case of the vice president—their limited public visibility and accountability.

In person Douglas Feith is nothing like Rasputin. Between a Reagan-era stint in the Pentagon and his current job he was a Washington lawyer for fifteen years, and he answered my questions with a lawyer's affability in the face of presumed disagreement. I could be biased in Feith's favor, because he was the most senior administration official who granted my request for an interview about postwar Iraq. Like Donald Rumsfeld, Feith acts and sounds younger than many others of his age (fifty). But distinctly unlike Rumsfeld at a press conference, Feith in this interview did not seem at all arrogant or testy. His replies were relatively candid and unforced, in contrast to the angry or relentlessly on-message responses that have become standard from senior administration officials. He acknowledged what was "becoming the conventional wisdom" about the administration's failure to plan adequately for events after the fall of Baghdad, and then explained—with animation, dramatic pauses, and gestures—why he thought it was wrong.

Feith offered a number of specific illustrations of what he considered underappreciated successes. Some were familiar—the oil wells weren't on fire, Iraqis didn't starve or flee—but others were less so. For instance, he described the Administration's careful effort to replace old Iraqi dinars, which carried Saddam Hussein's image ("It's interesting how important that is, and it ties into the whole issue of whether people think that Saddam might be coming back."), with a new form of currency, without causing a run on the currency.

But mainly he challenged the premise of most critics: that

the administration could have done a better job of preparing for the consequences of victory. When I asked what had gone better than expected, and what had gone worse, he said, "We don't exactly deal in 'expectations.' Expectations are too close to 'predictions.' We're not comfortable with predictions. It is one of the big strategic premises of the work that we do."

The limits of future knowledge, Feith said, were of special importance to Rumsfeld, "who is death to predictions." "His big strategic theme is uncertainty," Feith said. "The need to deal strategically with uncertainty. The inability to predict the future. The limits on our knowledge and the limits on our intelligence."

In practice, Feith said, this meant being ready for whatever proved to be the situation in postwar Iraq. "You will not find a single piece of paper . . . If anybody ever went through all of our records—and someday some people will, presumably—nobody will find a single piece of paper that says, 'Mr. Secretary or Mr. President, let us tell you what postwar Iraq is going to look like, and here is what we need plans for.' If you tried that, you would get thrown out of Rumsfeld's office so fast—if you ever went in there and said, 'Let me tell you what something's going to look like in the future,' you wouldn't get to your next sentence!

"This is an important point," he said, "because of this issue of 'What did we believe?' . . . The common line is, nobody planned for security because Ahmed Chalabi told us that everything was going to be swell." Chalabi, the exiled leader of the Iraqi National Congress, has often been blamed for making rosy predictions about the ease of governing postwar Iraq. "So we predicted that everything was going to be swell, and we didn't plan for things not being swell." Here Feith paused for a few seconds, raised his hands with both palms up, and put on a "Can you believe it?" expression. "I mean—one would really have to be a simpleton. And whatever people think of me, how can anybody think that Don Rumsfeld is that dumb? He's so evidently not that dumb, that how can people write things like that?" He sounded amazed rather than angry.

No one contends that Donald Rumsfeld, or Paul Wolfowitz, or Douglas Feith, or the administration as a whole is dumb. The wisdom of their preparations for the aftermath of military victory in Iraq is the question. Feith's argument was a less defensive-sounding version of the administration's general response to criticisms of its postwar policy: Life is uncertain, especially when the lid comes off a long-tyrannized society. American planners did about as well as anyone could in preparing for the unforeseeable. Anyone who says otherwise is indulging in lazy, unfair second-guessing. "The notion that there was a memo that was once written, that if we had only listened to that memo, all would be well in Iraq, is so preposterous," Feith told me.

The notion of a single memo's changing history is indeed far-fetched. The idea that a substantial body of knowledge could have improved postwar prospects is not. The administration could not have known everything about what it would find in Iraq. But it could have—and should have—done far more than it did.

Almost everything, good and bad, that has happened in Iraq since the fall of Saddam Hussein's regime was the subject of extensive prewar discussion and analysis. This is particularly true of what have proved to be the harshest realities for the United States since the fall of Baghdad: that occupying the country is much more difficult than conquering it; that a breakdown in public order can jeopardize every other goal; that the ambition of patiently nurturing a new democracy is at odds with the desire to turn control over to the Iraqis quickly and get U.S. troops out; that the Sunni center of the country is the main security problem; that with each passing day Americans risk being seen less as liberators and more as occupiers, and targets.

All this, and much more, was laid out in detail and in writing long before the U.S. government made the final decision to attack. Even now the collective efforts at planning by the CIA, the State Department, the U.S. Army and the Marine Corps, the United States Agency for International Development, and a wide variety of other groups inside and outside the government are underappreciated by the public. The one prewar effort that has received substantial recent attention, the State Department's Future of Iraq project, produced thousands of pages of findings, barely one paragraph of which has until now been quoted in the press.* The

---

*In the fall of 2003 an independent researcher named Russ Kick filed a request for documents produced by the Future of Iraq project, under the Freedom of Information Act. Nearly two and a half years later, in February 2006, the State Department granted the request and released more than one thousand pages of documents to Kick. He converted them to PDF files and made them available without charge at his Web site, TheMemoryHole.org. The report can be found at http://www. thememoryhole.org/state/future_of_iraq/.

administration will be admired in retrospect for how much knowledge it created about the challenge it was taking on. U.S. government predictions about postwar Iraq's problems have proved as accurate as the assessments of prewar Iraq's strategic threat have proved flawed.

But the administration will be condemned for what it did with what was known. The problems the United States has encountered are precisely the ones its own expert agencies warned against. Exactly what went wrong with the occupation will be studied for years—or should be. The missteps of the first half year in Iraq are as significant as other classic and carefully examined failures in foreign policy, including John Kennedy's handling of the Bay of Pigs invasion in 1961, and Lyndon Johnson's decision to escalate U.S. involvement in Vietnam in 1965. The United States withstood those previous failures, and it will withstand this one. Having taken over Iraq and captured Saddam Hussein, it has no moral or practical choice other than to see out the occupation and to help rebuild and democratize the country. But its missteps have come at a heavy cost. And the ongoing financial, diplomatic, and human cost of the Iraq occupation is the more grievous in light of advance warnings the government had.

BEFORE SEPTEMBER 11, 2001: THE EARLY DAYS

Concern about Saddam Hussein predated the 9/11 attacks and even the inauguration of George W. Bush. In 1998 Congress passed and President Bill Clinton signed the Iraq Liberation Act, which declared that "it should be the policy of the United States to support efforts to remove the regime headed by Saddam Hussein from power." During the 2000 presidential campaign Al Gore promised to support groups working to unseat Saddam Hussein. In the week before Bush took office, Nicholas Lemann reported in *The New Yorker* that "the idea of overthrowing Saddam is not an idle fantasy—or, if it is, it's one that has lately occupied the minds of many American officials, including people close to George W. Bush." But the intellectual case for regime change, argued during the Clinton years by some Democrats and notably by Paul Wolfowitz, then the dean of the Johns Hopkins School of Advanced International Studies, shifted clearly toward operational planning after the destruction of the World Trade Center.

For much of the public this case for war against Iraq rested on an assumed connection (though this was never demonstrated, and was officially disavowed by the president) between Saddam Hussein's regime and the terrorist hijackers. Within the government the case was equally compelling but different. September 11 had shown that the United States was newly vulnerable; to protect itself it had to fight terrorists at their source; and because Saddam Hussein's regime was the leading potential source of future "state-sponsored" terrorism, it had become an active threat, whether or not it played any role in 9/11.* The very next

---

*Years later, a version of this argument became the administration's primary public defense of the need for war. After postwar inspections of Iraq

day, September 12, 2001, James Woolsey, who had been Clinton's first CIA director, told me that no matter who proved to be responsible for this attack, the solution had to include removing Saddam Hussein, because he was so likely to be involved next time. A military planner inside the Pentagon later told me that on September 13, his group was asked to draw up scenarios for an assault on Iraq, not just Afghanistan.

Soon after becoming the army chief of staff in 1999, General Eric Shinseki had begun ordering war-game exercises to judge strategies and manpower needs for possible combat in Iraq. This was not because he assumed a war was imminent. He thought that the greater Caspian Sea region, including Iraq, would present a uniquely difficult challenge for U.S. troops, because of its geography and political tensions. After 9/11, army war games involving Iraq began in earnest.

---

had failed to discover signs of nuclear, biological, or chemical weapons programs, and when no strong evidence of a link between Saddam Hussein and the 9/11 hijackers emerged, the administration stressed that Iraq was in a deeper way tied to the vulnerability revealed on September 11, 2001. For instance, in his State of the Union Address in January 2006, President Bush introduced his discussion of Iraq this way:

> "On September the 11, 2001, we found that problems originating in a failed and oppressive state seven thousand miles away could bring murder and destruction to our country. Dictatorships shelter terrorists, and feed resentment and radicalism, and seek weapons of mass destruction. Democracies replace resentment with hope, respect the rights of their citizens and their neighbors, and join the fight against terror. Every step toward freedom in the world makes our country safer—so we will act boldly in freedom's cause."

In his first State of the Union address on January 29, 2002, President Bush said that Iraq, Iran, and North Korea were an "axis of evil" that threatened world peace. "By seeking weapons of mass destruction, these regimes pose a grave and growing danger. They could provide these arms to terrorists, giving them the means to match their hatred. They could attack our allies or attempt to blackmail the United States."

By the time of this speech efforts were afoot not simply to remove Saddam Hussein but also to imagine what Iraq would be like when he was gone. In late October 2001, while the U.S. military was conducting its rout of the Taliban from Afghanistan, the State Department had quietly begun its planning for the aftermath of a "transition" in Iraq. At about the time of the "axis of evil" speech, working groups within the department were putting together a list of postwar jobs and topics to be considered, and possible groups of experts to work on them.

ONE YEAR BEFORE THE WAR: THE "FUTURE OF IRAQ"

Thus was born the Future of Iraq project, whose existence is by now well known, but whose findings and potential impact have rarely been reported and examined. The State Department first publicly mentioned the project in March 2002, when it quietly announced the lineup of the working groups. At the time, media attention was overwhelmingly directed toward Afghanistan, where Operation Anaconda, the half-successful effort to kill or capture al-Qaeda and Taliban fighters, was under way.

For several months before announcing the project the State Department had been attempting to coordinate the efforts of the many fractious Iraqi exile organizations. The Future of Iraq project held the potential for harnessing, and perhaps even harmonizing, the expertise available from the exile groups.

It was also in keeping with a surprisingly well-established U.S. government tradition of preparing for postwar duties before there was a clear idea of when fighting would begin, let alone when it would end. Before the United States entered World War II, teams at the Army War College were studying what went right and wrong when American doughboys occupied Germany after World War I. Within months of the attack on Pearl Harbor a School of Military Government had been created, at the University of Virginia, to plan for the occupation of both Germany and Japan. In 1995, while U.S. negotiators, led by Richard Holbrooke, were still working at the Dayton peace talks to end the war in the Balkans, World Bank representatives were on hand to arrange loans for the new regimes.

Contemplating postwar plans posed a problem for those who, like many in the State Department, were skeptical of the need for war. Were they making a war more likely if they prepared for its aftermath? Thomas Warrick, the State Department official who directed the Future of Iraq project, was considered to be in the antiwar camp. But according to associates, he explained the importance of preparing for war by saying, "I'm nervous that they're actually going to do it—and the day after they'll turn to us and ask, 'Now what?'" So he pushed ahead with the project, setting up numerous conferences and drafting sessions that would bring together teams of exiles—among them Kanan Makiya, the author of the influential anti-Saddam book *Republic of Fear,* first published in 1989. A small number of "international advisers," mainly from the United States, were also assigned to the teams. Eventually there would be seventeen working groups, designed systematically to cover what would be needed to rebuild the political and economic infrastructure of the country. "Democratic Principles and Procedures" was the name of one of the groups, which was assigned to suggest the legal framework for a new government; Makiya would write much of its report. The "Transitional Justice" group was supposed to work on reparations, amnesty, and de-Baathification laws. Groups studying economic matters included "Public Finance," "Oil and Energy," and "Water, Agriculture, and Environment."

In May 2002 Congress authorized $5 million to fund the project's studies. In the flurry of news from Afghanistan the project went unnoticed in the press until June, when the State Department announced that the first meetings would take place in July. "The role of the U.S. government and State Department is to see what the Iraqis and Iraqi-Americans want," Warrick said at a conference on June 1, 2002. "The impetus for change comes from [Iraqis], not us. This is the job of Iraqis inside and outside."

That same day President Bush delivered a graduation speech at West Point, giving a first look at the doctrine of preemptive war. He told the cadets, to cheers, "Our security will require all Americans to be forward-looking and resolute, to be ready for preemptive action when necessary to defend our liberty and to defend our lives." Later in the summer the doctrine was elaborated in a new National Security Strategy, which explained that since "rogue states" could not be contained or deterred, they needed to be destroyed before they could attack.

Whenever National Security Adviser Condoleezza Rice was interviewed that summer, she talked mainly about the thinking behind the new policy. When Vice President Dick Cheney was interviewed, he talked mainly about Saddam Hussein's defiance of international law. But when Secretary of State Colin Powell was interviewed, he constantly stressed the value of an international approach to the problem and the need to give UN arms inspectors adequate time to do their job.

War with Iraq was not inevitable at this point, but it seemed more and more likely. Daily conversation in Washington, which usually reverts to "So, who do you think will be the next president?" switched instead to "So, when do you think we're going to war?"

It was in these circumstances that the Future of Iraq project's working groups deliberated. Most of the meetings were in Washington. Some were in London, and one session, in early September, took place in Surrey, where representatives of a dozen mutually suspicious exile groups discussed prospects for democratic coexistence when Saddam Hussein was gone. (Along with Chalabi's INC the meeting included several rival Kurdish groups, Assyrian and Turkomen organizations, the Iraqi Constitutional Monarchy Movement, and others.)

The project did not overcome all the tensions among its members, and the results of its deliberations were uneven. Three of its intended working groups never actually met— including, ominously, "Preserving Iraq's Cultural Heritage." The "Education" group finally produced a report only six pages long, in contrast to many hundreds of pages from most others. Some recommendations were quirky or reflected the tastes of the individual participants who drafted them. A report titled "Free Media" proposed that all Iraqi journalists be taken out of the country for a monthlong reeducation process: "Those who 'get it' go back as reporters; others would be retired or reassigned." A group that was considering ways of informing Iraq about the realities of democracy mentioned *Baywatch* and *Leave It to Beaver* as information sources that had given Iraqis an imprecise understanding of American society. It recommended that a new film, *Colonial America: Life in a Theocracy,* be shot, noting, "The Puritan experiments provide amazing parallels with current Moslem fundamentalism. The ultimate failures of these U.S. experiments can also be vividly illustrated—witch trials, intolerance, etc."

But whatever may have been unrealistic or factional about these efforts, even more of what the project created was impressive. The final report consisted of thirteen volumes of recommendations on specific topics, plus a one-volume summary and overview. These I have read—and I read them several months into the occupation, when it was unfairly easy to judge how well the forecast was standing up. (Several hundred of the 2,500 pages were in Arabic, which sped up the reading process.) The report was labeled "For Official Use Only"—an administrative term that implies confidentiality but has no legal significance. The State Department held the report closely until, last fall, it agreed to congressional requests to turn over the findings.

Most of the project's judgments look good in retrospect—and virtually all reveal a touching earnestness about working out the details of reconstructing a society. For instance, one of the thickest volumes considered the corruption endemic in Iraqi life and laid out strategies for coping with it. (These included a new "Iraqi Government Code of Ethics," which began, "Honesty, integrity, and fairness are the fundamental values for the people of Iraq.") The overview volume, which appears to have been composed as a series of PowerPoint charts, said that the United States was undertaking this effort because, among other things, "detailed public planning" conveys U.S. government "seriousness" and the message that the U.S. government "wants to learn from past regime-change experiences."

For their part, the Iraqi participants emphasized several points that ran through all the working groups' reports. A recurring theme was the urgency of restoring electricity and water supplies as soon as possible after regime change. The first item in the list of recommendations from the "Water,

Agriculture, and Environment" group read, "Fundamental importance of clean water supplies for Iraqis immediately after transition. Key to coalition/community relations." One of the groups making economic recommendations wrote, "Stressed importance of getting electrical grid up and running immediately—key to water systems, jobs. Could go a long way to determining Iraqis' attitudes toward Coalition forces."

A second theme was the need to plan carefully for the handling and demobilization of Iraq's very sizable military. On the one hand, a functioning army would be necessary for public order and, once coalition forces withdrew, for the country's defense. ("Our vision of the future is to build a democratic civil society. In order to make this vision a reality, we need to have an army that can work alongside this new society.") On the other hand, a large number of Saddam's henchmen would have to be removed. The trick would be to get rid of the leaders without needlessly alienating the ordinary troops—or leaving them without income. One group wrote, "All combatants who are included in the demobilization process must be assured by their leaders and the new government of their legal rights and that new prospects for work and education will be provided by the new system." Toward this end it laid out a series of steps the occupation authorities should take in the "disarmament, demobilization, and reintegration" process. Another group, in a paper on democratic principles, warned, "The decommissioning of hundreds of thousands of trained military personnel that [a rapid purge] implies could create social problems."

Next the working groups emphasized how disorderly Iraq would be soon after liberation, and how difficult it would be to get the country on the path to democracy—though that was where it had to go. "The removal of Saddam's regime will provide a power vacuum and create popular anxieties about the viability of all Iraqi institutions," a paper on rebuilding civil society said. "The traumatic and disruptive events attendant to the regime change will affect all Iraqis, both Saddam's conspirators and the general populace." Another report warned more explicitly that "the period immediately after regime change might offer these criminals the opportunity to engage in acts of killing, plunder, and looting." In the short term the occupying forces would have to prevent disorder. In the long term, according to a report written by Kanan Makiya, they would need to recognize that "the extent of the Iraqi totalitarian state, its absolute power and control exercised from Baghdad, not to mention the terror used to enforce compliance, cannot be overestimated in their impact on the Iraqi psyche and the attendant feeling of fear, weakness, and shame." Makiya continued, "These conditions and circumstances do not provide a strong foundation on which to build new institutions and a modern nation state."

Each of the preceding themes would seem to imply a long, difficult U.S. commitment in Iraq. America should view its involvement in Iraq, the summary report said, not as it had Afghanistan, which was left to stew in lightly supervised warlordism, but as it had Germany and Japan, which were rebuilt over many years. But nearly every working group stressed one other point: the military occupation itself had to be brief. "Note: Military government idea did not go down well," one chart in the summary volume said. The "Oil and Energy" group presented a "key concept": "Iraqis do not work for American contractors; Americans are seen assisting Iraqis."

Americans are often irritated by the illogic of "resentful dependence" by weaker states. South Koreans, for example, complain bitterly about U.S. soldiers in their country but would complain all the more bitterly if the soldiers were removed. The authors of the Future of Iraq report could by those standards also be accused of illogical thinking, in wanting U.S. support but not wanting U.S. control. Moreover, many of the project's members had a bias that prefigured an important source of postwar tension: they were exiles who considered themselves the likeliest beneficiaries if the United States transferred power to Iraqis quickly—even though, precisely because of their exile, they had no obvious base of support within Iraq.

To skip ahead in the story: As chaos increased in Baghdad during the summer of 2003, the chief U.S. administrator, L. Paul "Jerry" Bremer, wrestled constantly with a variant of this exile paradox. The Iraqi Governing Council, whose twenty-five members were chosen by Americans, was supposed to do only the preparatory work for an elected Iraqi government. But the greater the pressure on Bremer for "Iraqification," the more tempted he was to give in to the council's demand that he simply put it in charge without waiting for an election. More than a year earlier, long before combat began, the explicit recommendations and implicit lessons of the Future of Iraq project had given the U.S. government a very good idea of what political conflicts it could expect in Iraq.

TEN MONTHS BEFORE THE WAR:
WAR GAMES AND WARNINGS

As combat slowed in Afghanistan and the teams of the Future of Iraq project continued their deliberations, the U.S. government put itself on a wartime footing. In late May the CIA had begun what would become a long series of war-game exercises, to think through the best- and worst-case scenarios after the overthrow of Saddam Hussein. According to a person familiar with the process, one recurring theme in the exercises was the risk of civil disorder after the fall of Baghdad. The exercises explored how to find and secure the weapons of mass destruction that were then assumed to be in and around Baghdad, and indicated that the hardest task would be finding and protecting scientists who knew about the weapons before they could be killed by the regime as it was going down.

The CIA also considered whether a new Iraqi government could be put together through a process like the Bonn conference, which was then being used to devise a post-Taliban regime for Afghanistan. At the Bonn conference representatives of rival political and ethnic groups agreed on the terms that established Hamid Karzai as the new Afghan president.

The CIA believed that rivalries in Iraq were so deep, and the political culture so shallow, that a similarly quick transfer of sovereignty would only invite chaos.

Representatives from the Defense Department were among those who participated in the first of these CIA war-game sessions. When their Pentagon superiors at the Office of the Secretary of Defense (OSD) found out about this, in early summer, the representatives were reprimanded and told not to participate further. "OSD" is Washington shorthand, used frequently in discussions about the origins of Iraq war plans, and it usually refers to strong guidance from Rumsfeld, Wolfowitz, Feith, and one of Feith's deputies, William Luti. Their displeasure over the CIA exercise was an early illustration of a view that became stronger throughout 2002: that postwar planning was an impediment to war.

Because detailed thought about the postwar situation meant facing costs and potential problems, and thus weakened the case for launching a "war of choice" (the Washington term for a war not waged in immediate self-defense), it could be seen as an "antiwar" undertaking. The knowledge that U.S. soldiers would still be in Germany and Japan sixty-plus years after Pearl Harbor would obviously not have changed the decision to enter World War II, and in theory the Bush administration could have presented the overthrow of Saddam Hussein in a similar way: as a job that had to be done, even though it might saddle Americans with costs and a military presence for decades to come. Everyone can think of moments when Bush or Rumsfeld has reminded the nation that this would be a long-term challenge. But during the months when the administration was making its case for the war—successfully to Congress, less so to the United Nations—it acted as if the long run should be thought about only later on.

On July 31, 2002, the Senate Foreign Relations Committee invited a panel of experts to discuss the case for war against Iraq. On August 1 it heard from other experts about the likely "day after" consequences of military victory. Senator Joseph Biden, a Democrat from Delaware, was then the chairman of the committee. That first day Biden said that the threat of WMD might force him to vote in favor of the war (as he ultimately did). But he worried that if the United States invaded without full allied support, "we may very well radicalize the rest of the world; we may pick up a bill that's $70 billion, $80 billion; we may have to have extensive commitment of U.S. forces for an extended period of time in Iraq."

Phebe Marr, an Iraq scholar retired from the National Defense University, told the committee that the United States "should assume that it cannot get the results it wants on the cheap" from regime change. "It must be prepared to put some troops on the ground, advisers to help create new institutions, and above all, time and effort in the future to see the project through to a satisfactory end. If the United States is not willing to do so, it had best rethink the project." Rend Rahim Francke, an Iraqi exile serving on the Future of Iraq project (and now the ambassador from Iraq to the United States), said that "the system of public security will break down, because there will be no functioning police force, no civil service, and no justice system" on the first day after the fighting. "There will be a vacuum of political authority and administrative authority," she said. "The infrastructure of vital sectors will have to be restored. An adequate police force must be trained and equipped as quickly as possible. And the economy will have to be jump-started from not only stagnation but devastation."* Other witnesses discussed the need to commit U.S. troops for many years—but to begin turning constitutional authority over to the Iraqis within six months. The upshot of the hearings was an emphasis on the short-term importance of security, the medium-term challenge of maintaining control while transferring sovereignty to the Iraqis, and the long-term reality of commitments and costs. All the experts agreed that what came after the fall of Baghdad would be harder for the United States than what came before.

SIX MONTHS BEFORE THE WAR: GETTING SERIOUS

One week before Labor Day, while President Bush was at his ranch in Texas, Vice President Cheney gave a speech at a

---

*As became evident after the war, other organizations and experts were also warning in the summer and fall of 2002 about the risk of looting and public disorder after Saddam Hussein was deposed. But most of their work was classified or not publicly available at the time. Phebe Marr's statement at a nationally televised hearing was one of the clearest public statements before the war about the need to ensure order once the war began.

Veterans of Foreign Wars convention in Nashville. "There is no doubt that Saddam Hussein now has weapons of mass destruction [and that he will use them] against our friends, against our allies, and against us," Cheney said. Time was running out, he concluded, for America to remove this threat. A few days later CNN quoted a source "intimately familiar with [Colin] Powell's thinking" as saying that Powell was still insistent on the need for allied support and would oppose any war in which the United States would "go it alone . . . as if it doesn't give a damn" about other nations' views.* Just after Labor Day, Powell apparently won a battle inside the administration and persuaded Bush to take the U.S. case to the United Nations. On September 12 Bush addressed the UN General Assembly and urged it to insist on Iraqi compliance with its previous resolutions concerning disarmament.

Before the war the administration exercised remarkable "message discipline" about financial projections. When

---

*In retrospect these reported comments by Cheney and Powell in the late summer of 2002 are striking for the way each man perfectly fits his expected dramatic and rhetorical role. The vice president is unyielding, as always. There is "no doubt" that Iraq has developed weapons of mass destruction, as at other times there was no doubt that American soldiers would be greeted "with flowers" in Iraq or that Iraq's insurgents were "on their last legs." Meanwhile, the then–Secretary of State stood by the administration's policy in public while copiously signaling via press leaks his private misgivings and doubts.

Powell's inside-outside role made his reputation another casualty of the Iraq war. Bob Woodward's accounts, bolstered by the revelations in late 2005 of Powell's former State Department chief of staff, Lawrence

asked how much the war might cost, officials said that so many things were uncertain, starting with whether there would even be a war, that there was no responsible way to make an estimate. In part this reflected Rumsfeld's emphasis on the unknowability of the future. It was also politically essential, in delaying the time when the administration had to argue that regime change in Iraq was worth a specific number of billions of dollars.

In September, Lawrence Lindsay, then the chief White House economic adviser, broke discipline. He was asked by *The Wall Street Journal* how much a war and its aftermath might cost. He replied that it might end up at 1 to 2 percent of the gross domestic product, which would mean $100 billion to $200 billion. Lindsay added that he thought the cost of not going to war could conceivably be greater—but that didn't placate his critics within the administration. The administration was further annoyed by a report a few days later from Democrats on the House Budget Committee,

---

Wilkerson, portray Powell as having foreseen many of the political, military, and diplomatic failings of the administration's strategy in Iraq. But Powell never indicated any of this publicly, in his own name, when it might have made a difference. Also in retrospect, it seems that there were two men whose opposition might have affected America's decision to go to war in March 2003. One was Tony Blair, whose support for the war was crucial to the Bush administration both domestically and internationally. The other was Powell, who threw his considerable prestige behind the case for war with his presentation to the United Nations Security Council in February 2003. The difference between Blair's situation and Powell's is that, based on all available evidence, Tony Blair sincerely believed in the need for war in Iraq, whereas Colin Powell did not.

which estimated the cost of the war at $48 billion to $93 billion. Lindsay was widely criticized in "background" comments from administration officials, and by the end of the year he had been forced to resign. His comment "made it clear Larry just didn't get it," an unnamed administration official told *The Washington Post* when Lindsay left. Lindsay's example could hardly have encouraged others in the administration to be forthcoming with financial projections. Indeed, no one who remained in the administration offered a plausible cost estimate until months after the war began.

In September the United States Agency for International Development began to think in earnest about its postwar responsibilities in Iraq. It was the natural contact for nongovernmental organizations, or NGOs, from the United States and other countries that were concerned with relief efforts in Iraq.

USAID's administrator, Andrew Natsios, came to the assignment with a complex set of experiences and instincts. He started his career, in the 1970s, as a Republican state legislator in Massachusetts, and before the Bush administration he had been the administrator of the state's "Big Dig," the largest public-works effort ever in the country. Before the Big Dig, Natsios spent five years as an executive at a major humanitarian NGO called World Vision. He also served in the Persian Gulf during the 1991 Gulf War, as an Army Reserve officer. By background he was the administration official best prepared to anticipate the combination of wartime and postwar obligations in Iraq.

At any given moment USAID is drawing up contingency plans for countries that might soon need help. "I actually have a list, which I will not show you," Natsios told me in the fall, "of countries where there may not be American troops soon, but they could fall apart—and if they do, what we could do for them." By mid-September 2002, six months before the official beginning of Operation Iraqi Freedom, Natsios had additional teams working on plans for Iraq. Representatives of about a dozen relief organizations and NGOs were gathering each week at USAID headquarters for routine coordination meetings. Iraq occupied more and more of their time through 2002. On October 10, one day before Congress voted to authorize the war, the meetings were recast as the Iraq Working Group.

FIVE MONTHS BEFORE THE WAR:
OCCUPIERS OR LIBERATORS?

The weekly meetings at USAID quickly settled into a pattern. The representatives of the NGOs would say, "We've dealt with situations like this before, and we know what to expect." The U.S. government representatives would either say nothing or else reply, "No, this time it will be different."

The NGOs had experience dealing with a reality that has not fully sunk in for most of the American public. In the nearly three decades since U.S. troops left Vietnam, the American military has fought only two wars as most people understand the term: the two against Saddam Hussein's Iraq. But through the past thirty years U.S. troops have almost continuously been involved in combat somewhere. Because those engagements—in Grenada, Lebanon, Panama, Haiti,

Somalia, Bosnia, Kosovo, Afghanistan, and elsewhere—have no obvious connection with one another, politicians and the public usually discuss them as stand-alone cases. Each one seems an aberration from the "real" wars the military is set up to fight.

To the NGO world, these and other modern wars (like the ones in Africa) are not the exception but the new norm: brutal localized encounters that destroy the existing political order and create a need for long-term international supervision and support. Within the U.S. military almost no one welcomes this reality, but many recognize that peace-keeping, policing, and, yes, nation-building are now the expected military tasks. The military has gotten used to working alongside the NGOs—and the NGOs were ready with a checklist of things to worry about once the regime had fallen.

An even larger question about historical precedent began to surface. When administration officials talked about models for what would happen in Iraq, they almost always referred to the lasting success in Japan and Germany—or else to countries of the former Soviet bloc in Eastern Europe. (A civilian adviser who went to Baghdad early in the occupation recalls looking at his fellow passengers on the military transport plane. The ones who weren't asleep or flipping through magazines were reading books about Japan or Germany, not about the Arab world. "That was not a good sign," he told me.) If one thought of Iraq as Poland, or as the former East Germany, or as the former Czechoslovakia, or as almost any part of the onetime Soviet empire in Eastern Europe other than Romania, one would naturally conclude that regime change in itself would set the country well along the path toward recovery. These countries were fine once their repressive leaders were removed; so might Iraq well be. And if the former Yugoslavia indicated darker possibilities, that could be explained as yet another failure of Clinton-era foreign policy.

Many NGO representatives assumed that postwar recovery would not be so automatic, and that they should begin working on preparations before the combat began. "At the beginning our main message was the need for access," I was told by Sandra Mitchell, the vice president of the International Rescue Committee (IRC), who attended the USAID meetings. Because of U.S. sanctions against Iraq, it was illegal for American humanitarian organizations to operate there. (Journalists were about the only category of Americans who would not get in trouble with their own government by traveling to and spending money in Iraq.) "Our initial messages were like those in any potential crisis situation," Mitchell said, "but the reason we were so insistent in this case was the precarious situation that already existed in Iraq. The internal infrastructure was shot, and you couldn't easily swing in resources from neighboring countries, like in the Balkans." The NGOs therefore asked, as a first step, for a presidential directive exempting them from the sanctions. They were told to expect an answer to this request by December. That deadline passed with no ruling. By the beginning of 2003 the NGOs felt that it was too dangerous to go to Iraq, and the administration feared that if they went they might be used as hostages. No directive was ever issued.

Through the fall and winter of 2002 the International

Rescue Committee, Refugees International, InterAction, and other groups that met with USAID kept warning about one likely postwar problem that, as it turned out, Iraq avoided—a mass flow of refugees—and another that was exactly as bad as everyone warned: the lawlessness and looting of the "day after" in Baghdad. The Bush administration would later point to the absence of refugees as a sign of the occupation's underreported success. This achievement was, indeed, due in part to a success: the speed and precision of the military campaign itself. But the absence of refugees was also a sign of a profound failure: the mistaken estimates of Iraq's WMD threat. All prewar scenarios involving huge movements of refugees began with the assumption that Saddam Hussein would use chemical or biological weapons against U.S. troops or his own Kurdish or Shiite populations—and that either the fact or the fear of such assaults would force terrified Iraqis to evacuate.

The power vacuum that led to looting was disastrous. "The looting was not a surprise," Sandra Mitchell told me. "It should not have come as a surprise. Anyone who has witnessed the fall of a regime while another force is coming in on a temporary basis knows that looting is standard procedure. In Iraq there were very strong signals that this could be the period of greatest concern for humanitarian response." One lesson of postwar reconstruction through the 1990s was that even a short period of disorder could have long-lasting effects.

The meetings at USAID gave the veterans of international relief operations a way to register their concerns. The problem was that they heard so little back. "The people in front of us were very well-meaning," says Joel Charny, who represented Refugees International at the meetings. "And in fairness, they were on such a short leash. But the dialogue was one-way. We would tell them stuff, and they would nod and say, 'Everything's under control.' To me it was like the old four-corners offense in basketball. They were there to just dribble out the clock but be able to say they'd consulted with us."

And again the question arose of whether what lay ahead in Iraq would be similar to the other "small wars" of the previous decade-plus or something new. If it was similar, the NGOs had their checklists ready. These included, significantly, the obligations placed on any "occupying power" by the Fourth Geneva Convention, which was signed in 1949 and is mainly a commonsense list of duties—from protecting hospitals to minimizing postwar reprisals—that a victorious army must carry out. "But we were corrected when we raised this point," Sandra Mitchell says. "The American troops would be 'liberators' rather than 'occupiers,' so the obligations did not apply. Our point was not to pass judgment on the military action but to describe the responsibilities."

In the same mid-October week that the Senate approved the war resolution, a team from the Strategic Studies Institute at the Army War College, in Carlisle Barracks, Pennsylvania, began a postwar-planning exercise. Even more explicitly than the NGOs, the army team insisted that America's military past, reaching back to its conquest of the Philippines, in 1898, would be a useful guide to its future duties in Iraq. As a rule, professional soldiers spend more time thinking and talking about history than other people do; past battles are the only real evidence about doctrine and equipment. The institute—in essence, the War College's think tank—was charged with reviewing recent occupations to help the army "best address the requirements that will necessarily follow operational victory in a war with Iraq," as the institute's director later said in a foreword to the team's report. "As the possibility of war with Iraq looms on the horizon, it is important to look beyond the conflict to the challenges of occupying the country."

The study's principal authors were Conrad Crane, who graduated from West Point in the early 1970s* and taught there as a history professor through the 1990s, and Andrew Terrill, an Army Reserve officer and a strategic-studies pro-

---

*A number of Crane's classmates from the West Point class of 1974 also played prominent roles in setting and implementing policy concerning Iraq. They include three-star generals Dave Petraeus, whose approach to training Iraqi soldiers in 2004 and 2005 is discussed in the fourth chapter of this book; Martin Dempsey, his successor in that job; Keith Alexander, who became director of the National Security Agency in 2005; and Walter Sharp, who was director of Strategic Plans and Policy for the Joint Chiefs of Staff during the war in Iraq and became director of the entire Joint Staff in 2005. Another classmate, two-star general William Webster, took command of the Army's Third Infantry Division in Iraq in the fall of 2003. Yet another, two-star general John Batiste, was a military advisor to Paul Wolfowitz in 2001 and commanded the Army's First infantry Division in Iraq in 2004. In the summer of 2005, just before he was to take a new assignment that would have led to a third star, Batiste resigned from the army. In 2006 he was one of the retired generals who called for Donald Rumsfeld's resignation.

fessor. With a team of other researchers, which included representatives from the army and the Joint Staff as well as other government agencies and think tanks, they began high-speed work on a set of detailed recommendations about postwar priorities. The Army War College report was also connected to a prewar struggle with yet another profound postwar consequence: the fight within the Pentagon, between the civilian leadership in OSD and the generals running the army, over the size and composition of the force that would conquer Iraq.

FOUR MONTHS BEFORE THE WAR:
THE BATTLE IN THE PENTAGON

On November 5, 2002, the Republicans regained control of the Senate and increased their majority in the House in national midterm elections. On November 8 the UN Security Council voted 15–0 in favor of Resolution 1441, threatening Iraq with "serious consequences" if it could not prove that it had abandoned its weapons programs.

Just before 9/11 Donald Rumsfeld had been thought of as standing on a banana peel. The newspapers were full of leaked anonymous complaints from military officials who thought that his efforts to streamline and "transform" the Pentagon were unrealistic and damaging. But with his dramatic metamorphosis from embattled secretary of defense to triumphant secretary of war, Rumsfeld's reputation outside the administration and his influence within it rose. He was operating from a position of great power when, in November, he decided to "cut the TPFDD."

"Tipfid" is how people in the military pronounce the acronym for "time-phased force and deployment data," but what it really means to the armed forces, in particular the army, is a way of doing business that is methodical, careful, and sure. The TPFDD for Iraq was an unbelievably complex master plan governing which forces would go where, when, and with what equipment, on which planes or ships, so that everything would be coordinated and ready at the time of attack. One reason it took the military six months to get set for each of its wars against Iraq, a comparatively pitiful foe, was the thoroughness of TPFDD planning. To its supporters, this approach is old-school in the best sense: if you fight, you really fight. To its detractors, this approach is simply old—ponderous, inefficient, and, although they don't dare call it cowardly, risk-averse at the least.

A streamlined approach had proved successful in Afghanistan, at least for a while, as a relatively small U.S. force left much of the ground fighting to the Northern Alliance. In the longer run the American strategy created complications for Afghanistan, because the victorious Northern Alliance leaders were newly legitimized as warlords. Donald Rumsfeld was one member of the administration who seemed still to share the pre-9/11 suspicion about the risks of nation-building, and so didn't much care about the postwar consequences of a relatively small invasion force. (His deputy, Paul Wolfowitz, was more open to the challenge of rebuilding Iraq, but he would never undercut or disobey Rumsfeld.) In November, Rumsfeld began working through the

TPFDD, with the goal of paring the force planned for Iraq to its leanest, lightest acceptable level.

The war games run by the army and the Pentagon's Joint Staff had led to very high projected troop levels. The army's recommendation was for an invasion force 400,000 strong, made up of as many Americans as necessary and as many allied troops as possible. "All the numbers we were coming up with were quite large," Thomas White, a retired general (and former Enron executive) who was the secretary of the army during the war, told me recently. But Rumsfeld's idea of the right force size was more like 75,000. The army and the military's joint leadership moderated their requests in putting together the TPFDD, but Rumsfeld began challenging the force numbers in detail. When combat began, slightly more than 200,000 U.S. soldiers were massed around Iraq.

"In what I came to think of as Secretary Rumsfeld's style," an army official who was involved in the process told me recently, "he didn't directly say no but asked a lot of hard questions about the plan and sent us away without approval. He would ask questions that delayed the activation of units, because he didn't think the planned flow was right. Our people came back with the understanding that their numbers were far too big and they should be thinking more along the lines of Afghanistan"—that is, plan for a light, mobile attack featuring Special Forces soldiers. Another participant described Rumsfeld as looking line by line at the deployments proposed in the TPFDD and saying, "Can't we do this with one company?" or "Shouldn't we get rid of this unit?" Making detailed, last-minute adjustments to the TPFDD was, in the army's view, like pulling cogs at random out of a machine. According to an observer, "The generals would say, Sir, these changes will ripple back to every railhead and every company."

The longer-term problem involved what would happen after Baghdad fell, as it inevitably would. This was distinctly an army rather than a general military concern. "Where's the air force now?" an army officer asked rhetorically last fall. "They're back on their bases—and they're better off, since they don't need to patrol the 'no-fly' zones [in northern and southern Iraq, which U.S. warplanes had patrolled since the end of the Gulf War]. The navy's gone, and most of the marines have been pulled back. It's the army holding the sack of shit." A related concern involved what a long-term commitment to Iraq would do to the army's "ops tempo," or pace of operations—especially if Reserve and National Guard members, who had no expectations of long-term foreign service when they signed up, were posted in Iraq for months or even years.

The military's fundamental argument for building up what Rumsfeld considered a wastefully large force is that it would be even more useful after Baghdad fell than during actual combat. The first few days or weeks after the fighting, in this view, were crucial in setting long-term expectations. Civilians would see that they could expect a rapid return to order, and would behave accordingly—or they would see the opposite. This was the "shock and awe" that really mattered, in the army's view: the ability to make clear who was in charge. "Insights from successful occupations suggest that it is best to go in real heavy and then draw down fast,"

Conrad Crane, of the Army War College, told me. That is, a larger force would be necessary during and immediately after the war, but might mean a much smaller occupation presence six months later.

"We're in Baghdad, the regime is toppled—what's next?" Thomas White told me, recounting discussions before the war. One of the strongest advocates of a larger force was General Eric Shinseki, the army chief of staff. White said, "Guys like Shinseki, who had been in Bosnia [where he supervised the NATO force], been in Kosovo, started running the numbers and said, 'Let's assume the world is linear.' For five million Bosnians we had two hundred thousand people to watch over them. Now we have twenty-five million Iraqis to worry about, spread out over a state the size of California. How many people is this going to take?" The heart of the army's argument was that with too few soldiers, the United States would win the war only to be trapped in an untenable position during the occupation.

A note of personal rancor complicated these discussions, as it did many disagreements over postwar plans. In our interview Douglas Feith played this down—maintaining that press reports had exaggerated the degree of quarreling and division inside the administration. These reports, he said, mainly reflected the experience of lower-level officials who were embroiled in one specific policy area and "might find themselves pretty much always at odds with their counterparts from another agency." Higher up, where one might be "fighting with someone on one issue but allied with them on something else," relations were more collegial. Perhaps so.

But there was no concealing the hostility within the Pentagon between most uniformed leaders, especially in the army, and the civilians in OSD.

Donald Rumsfeld viewed Shinseki as a symbol of uncooperative, old-style thinking, and had in the past gone out of his way to humiliate him.* In the spring of 2002, fourteen months before the scheduled end of Shinseki's term, Rumsfeld announced who his successor would be; such an announcement, which converts the incumbent into a lame duck, usually comes at the last minute. The action was one of several calculated insults.

From OSD's point of view, Shinseki and many of his colleagues were dragging their feet. From the army's point of view, OSD was being reckless about the way it was committing troops and high-handed in disregarding the military's professional advice. One man who was then working in the Pentagon told me of walking down a hallway a few months before the war and seeing Army General John Abizaid standing outside a door. Abizaid, who after the war succeeded Tommy Franks as commander of the Central Com-

---

*Had it not been for the publicized showdown between Shinseki and Rumsfeld's deputy, Paul Wolfowitz, described on pages 97–99 of this book, Rumsfeld might have gotten a more reasoned hearing for his argument that Shinseki and his army colleagues were too slow-moving and conventionally minded to fit his "transformation" plans. But in his public dressing-down of Shinseki, Wolfowitz was so high-handed, and so completely wrong, that he effectively immunized Shinseki against criticism of any sort.

For the record, despite numerous attempts over more than a year, I never succeeded in interviewing Shinseki himself. The accounts of his words and actions here come from others involved in the events described.

mand, or CentCom, was then the director of the Joint Staff—the highest uniformed position in the Pentagon apart from the Joint Chiefs. A planning meeting for Iraq operations was under way. OSD officials told him he could not take part.

The military-civilian difference finally turned on the question of which would be harder: winning the war or maintaining the peace. According to Thomas White and several others, OSD acted as if the war itself would pose the real challenge. As White put it, "The planning assumptions were that the people would realize they were liberated, they would be happy that we were there, so it would take a much smaller force to secure the peace than it did to win the war. The resistance would principally be the remnants of the Baath Party, but they would go away fairly rapidly. And, critically, if we didn't damage the infrastructure in our military operation, as we didn't, the restart of the country could be done fairly rapidly." The first assumption was clearly expressed by Cheney three days before the war began, in an exchange with Tim Russert on *Meet the Press:*

RUSSERT: If your analysis is not correct, and we're not treated as liberators but as conquerors, and the Iraqis begin to resist, particularly in Baghdad, do you think the American people are prepared for a long, costly, and bloody battle with significant American casualties?

CHENEY: Well, I don't think it's likely to unfold that way, Tim, because I really do believe that we will be greeted as liberators . . . The read we get on the people of Iraq is there is no question but what they want to get rid of Saddam Hussein and they will welcome as liberators the United States when we come to do that.

Through the 1990s Marine General Anthony Zinni, who preceded Tommy Franks as CentCom commander, had done war-gaming for a possible invasion of Iraq. His exercises involved a much larger U.S. force than the one that actually attacked in 2003. "They were very proud that they didn't have the kind of numbers my plan had called for," Zinni told me, referring to Rumsfeld and Cheney. "The reason we had those two extra divisions was the security situation. Revenge killings, crime, chaos—this was all foreseeable."

Thomas White agrees. Because of reasoning like Cheney's, "we went in with the minimum force to accomplish the military objectives, which was a straightforward task, never really in question," he told me. "And then we immediately found ourselves shorthanded in the aftermath. We sat there and watched people dismantle and run off with the country, basically."

THREE MONTHS BEFORE THE WAR

In the beginning of December 2002, Iraq submitted its 12,000-page declaration to the UN Security Council contending that it had no remaining WMD stores. Near the end of December, President Bush authorized the dispatch of more than 200,000 U.S. soldiers to the Persian Gulf.

There had still been few or no estimates of the war's cost from the administration—only contentions that projections like Lawrence Lindsay's were too high. When pressed on this point, administration officials repeatedly said that with so many uncertainties, they could not possibly estimate the cost. But early in December, just before Lindsay was forced out, *The New York Review of Books* published an article by William Nordhaus titled "Iraq: The Economic Conseequences of War," which included carefully considered estimates. Nordhaus, an economist at Yale, had served on Jimmy Carter's Council of Economic Advisers; the article was excerpted from a much longer economic paper he had prepared. His range of estimates was enormous, depending on how long the war lasted and what its impact on the world economy proved to be. Nordhaus calculated that over the course of a decade the direct and indirect costs of the war to the United States could be as low as $121 billion or as high as $1.6 trillion. This was a more thoroughgoing approach than the congressional budget committees had taken, but it was similar in its overall outlook. Nordhaus told me recently that he thinks he should have increased all his estimates to account for the "opportunity costs" of stationing soldiers in Iraq—that is, if they are assigned to Iraq, they're not available for deployment somewhere else.*

On the last day of December, Mitch Daniels, the director

---

*Even though such estimates are largely guesswork while a war is still underway, it appears that Nordhaus's estimate will be much closer to the ultimate figure than was any prediction from any administration official. In

of the Office of Management and Budget, told *The New York Times* that the war might cost $50 billion to $60 billion. He had to backtrack immediately, his spokesman stressing that "it is impossible to know what any military campaign would ultimately cost." The spokesman explained Daniels's mistake by saying, "The only cost estimate we know of in this arena is the Persian Gulf War, and that was a sixty-billion-dollar event." Daniels would leave the administration, of his own volition, five months later.

In the immediate run-up to the war the administration still insisted that the costs were unforeseeable. "Fundamentally, we have no idea what is needed unless and until we get there on the ground," Paul Wolfowitz told the House Budget Committee on February 27, with combat less than three weeks away. "This delicate moment—when we are assembling a coalition, when we are mobilizing people inside Iraq and throughout the region to help us in the event of war, and when we are still trying, through the United Nations and by other means, to achieve a peaceful solution without war—is not a good time to publish highly suspect numerical estimates and have them drive our declaratory policy."

Wolfowitz's stonewalling that day was in keeping with

January 2006, Joseph Stiglitz of Columbia and Linda Bilmes of Harvard's Kennedy School took an approach roughly similar to Nordhaus's three years earlier, in trying to assess all the direct and indirect costs (and benefits) of the war in Iraq. The final figure depended heavily on initial assumptions, but Stiglitz and Bilmes said the ultimate economic cost would likely be between $1 trillion and $2 trillion. Their paper is available at http://ksghome.harvard.edu/~lbilmes/paper/iraqnew.pdf

the policy of all senior administration officials. Until many months after combat had begun, they refused to hazard even the vaguest approximation of what financial costs it might involve. Shinseki, so often at odds with OSD, contemplated taking a different course. He was scheduled to testify, with Thomas White, before the Senate Appropriations Committee on March 19, which turned out to be the first day of actual combat. In a routine prep session before the hearing he asked his assistants what he should say about how much the operations in Iraq were going to cost. "Well, it's impossible to predict," a briefer began, reminding him of the official line.

Shinseki cut him off. "We don't know everything," he said, and then he went through a list of the many things the military already did know. "We know how many troops are there now, and the projected numbers. We know how much it costs to feed them every day. We know how much it cost to send the force there. We know what we have spent already to prepare the force and how much it would cost to bring them back. We have estimates of how much fuel and ammunition we would use per day of operations." In short, anyone who actually wanted to make an estimate had plenty of information on hand.

At this point Jerry Sinn, a three-star general in charge of the army's budget, said that in fact he had worked up some numbers—and he named a figure, for the army's likely costs, in the tens of billions of dollars. But when Senator Byron Dorgan, of North Dakota, asked Shinseki at hearings on March 19 how much the war just beginning would cost,

Shinseki was loyally vague ("Any potential discussion about what an operation in Iraq or any follow-on probably is undefined at this point").

When administration officials stopped being vague, they started being unrealistic. On March 27, eight days into combat, members of the House Appropriations Committee asked Paul Wolfowitz for a figure. He told them that whatever it was, Iraq's oil supplies would keep it low. "There's a lot of money to pay for this," he said. "It doesn't have to be U.S. taxpayer money. We are dealing with a country that can really finance its own reconstruction, and relatively soon." On April 23 Andrew Natsios, of USAID, told an incredulous Ted Koppel, on *Nightline,* that the total cost to America of reconstructing Iraq would be $1.7 billion. Koppel shot back, "I mean, when you talk about one-point-seven, you're not suggesting that the rebuilding of Iraq is gonna be done for one-point-seven billion dollars?" Natsios was clear: "Well, in terms of the American taxpayers' contribution, I do; this is it for the United States. The rest of the rebuilding of Iraq will be done by other countries who have already made pledges . . . But the American part of this will be one-point-seven billion dollars. We have no plans for any further-on funding for this."* Only in September did Presi-

---

*Natsios was a capable administrator of USAID, from which he resigned as director at the end of 2005 to join the faculty of Georgetown University. But because of its specificity, his assertion to Koppel stands out as the most wildly inaccurate prediction made by a government official before the war began. The figure he gave for the total "American part of this" proved to be off by a factor of at least several hundred.

dent Bush make his request for a supplemental appropria-
tion of $87 billion for operations in Iraq.

Planning for the postwar period intensified in December.
The Council on Foreign Relations, working with the Baker
Institute for Public Policy, at Rice University, convened a
working group on "guiding principles for U.S. postwar conflict policy in Iraq." Leslie Gelb, then the president of the
Council on Foreign Relations, said that the group would
take no position for or against the war. But its report, which
was prepared late in January of 2003 said that "U.S. and
coalition military units will need to pivot quickly from combat
to peacekeeping operations in order to prevent postconflict
Iraq from descending into anarchy." The report continued,
"Without an initial and broad-based commitment to law and
order, the logic of score-settling and revenge-taking will reduce Iraq to chaos."

The momentum toward war put officials at the United
Nations and other international organizations in a difficult
position. On the one hand, they had to be ready for what
was coming; on the other, it was awkward to be seen discussing the impending takeover of one of their member
states by another. "Off-the-record meetings were happening
in every bar in New York," one senior UN official told me in
the fall. An American delegation that included Pentagon
representatives went to Rome in December for a confidential meeting with officials of the UN's World Food Pro-
gramme (WFP), to discuss possible food needs after combat
in Iraq. As *The Wall Street Journal* later reported, the meeting was uncomfortable for both sides: the Americans had to

tell the WFP officials, as one of them recalled, "It is looking most probable you are going to witness one of the largest military engagements since the Second World War." This was hyperbole (Korea? Vietnam?), but it helped to convince the WFP that relief preparations should begin.

On December 11 an ice storm hit the mid-Atlantic states. For Conrad Crane and his associates at the Army War College, deep in their crash effort to prepare their report on postwar army challenges, this was a blessing. "The storm worked out perfectly," Crane told me afterward. "We were all on the post, there was no place anyone could go, we basically had the whole place to ourselves."

By the end of the month the War College team had assembled a draft of its report, called "Reconstructing Iraq: Insights, Challenges, and Missions for Military Forces in a Post-Conflict Scenario." It was not classified, and can be found through the Army War College's Web site.

The War College report has three sections. The first is a review of twentieth-century occupations—from the major efforts in Japan and Germany to the smaller and more recent ones in Haiti, Panama, and the Balkans. The purpose of the review is to identify common situations that occupiers might face in Iraq. The discussion of Germany, for instance, includes a detailed account of how U.S. occupiers "denazified" the country without totally dismantling its bureaucracy or excluding everyone who had held a position of responsibility. (The main tool was a *Fragebogen,* or questionnaire, about each person's past activities, which groups of anti-Nazi Germans and Allied investigators reviewed and based decisions on.)

The second section of the report is an assessment of the specific problems likely to arise in Iraq, given its ethnic and regional tensions and the impact of decades of Baathist rule. Most Iraqis would welcome the end of Saddam Hussein's tyranny, it said. Nonetheless,

> long-term gratitude is unlikely and suspicion of U.S. motives will increase as the occupation continues. A force initially viewed as liberators can rapidly be relegated to the status of invaders should an unwelcome occupation continue for a prolonged time. Occupation problems may be especially acute if the United States must implement the bulk of the occupation itself rather than turn these duties over to a postwar international force.

If these views about the risk of disorder and the short welcome that Americans would enjoy sound familiar, that is because every organization that looked seriously into the situation sounded the same note.

The last and most distinctive part of the War College report is its "Mission Matrix"—a 135-item checklist of what tasks would have to be done right after the war and by whom. About a quarter of these were "critical tasks" for which the military would have to be prepared long before it reached Baghdad: securing the borders so that foreign terrorists would not slip in (as they in fact did), locating and destroying WMD supplies, protecting religious sites, performing police and security functions, and so on. The matrix was intended to lay out a phased shift of responsibilities, over months or years, from a mainly U.S. occupation force to international organizations and, finally, to sovereign Iraqis. By the end of December copies of the War College report were being circulated throughout the army.

According to the standard military model, warfare unfolds through four phases: "deterrence and engagement," "seize the initiative," "decisive operations," and "postconflict." Reality is never divided quite that neatly, of course, but the War College report stressed that Phase IV "postconflict" planning absolutely had to start as early as possible, well before Phase III "decisive operations"—the war itself. But neither the army nor the other services moved very far past Phase III thinking. "All the A-Team guys wanted to be in on Phase III, and the B-Team guys were put on Phase IV," one man involved in Phase IV told me. Frederick Barton, of the Center for Strategic and International Studies, who was involved in postwar efforts in Haiti, Rwanda, and elsewhere, put it differently. "If you went to the Pentagon before the war, all the concentration was on the war," he said. "If you went there during the war, all the concentration was on the war. And if you went there after the war, they'd say, 'That's Jerry Bremer's job.'" Still, the War College report confirmed what the army leadership already suspected: that its real challenges would begin when it took control of Baghdad.

TWO MONTHS BEFORE THE WAR

On January 27, 2003, the chief UN weapons inspector, Hans Blix, reported that "Iraq appears not to have come to a genuine acceptance, not even today, of the disarmament that was demanded of it." Twenty-four hours later, in his State of the Union address, President Bush said that the United States was still hoping for UN endorsement of an action against Iraq—but would not be limited by the absence of one.

Increasingly the question in Washington about war was When? Those arguing for delay said that it would make everything easier. Perhaps Saddam Hussein would die. Perhaps he would flee or be overthrown. Perhaps the UN inspectors would find his weapons, or determine conclusively that they no longer existed. Perhaps the United States would have time to assemble, if not a broad alliance for the battle itself, at least support for reconstruction and occupation, so that U.S. soldiers and taxpayers would not be left with the entire job. Even if the responsibility were to be wholly America's, each passing month would mean more time to plan the peace as thoroughly as the war: to train civil-affairs units (which specialize in peacekeeping rather than combat), and to hire Arabic speakers. Indeed, several months into the U.S. occupation a confidential army "lessons learned" study said that the "lack of competent interpreters" throughout Iraq had "impeded operations." Most of the "military linguists" who were operating in Iraq, the study said, "basically [had] the ability to tell the difference between a burro and a burrito."

Those arguing against delay said that the mere passage of time wouldn't do any good and would bring various risks. The world had already waited twelve years since the Gulf War for Saddam Hussein to disarm. Congress had already voted to endorse the war. The Security Council had already shown its resolve. The troops were already on their way. Each passing day, in this view, was a day in which Saddam Hussein might deploy his weapons of terror.

Early in January the National Intelligence Council, at the CIA, ran a two-day exercise on postwar problems. Pentagon representatives were still forbidden by OSD to attend. The exercise covered issues similar to those addressed in the Future of Iraq and Army War College reports—and, indeed, to those considered by the Council on Foreign Relations and the Senate Foreign Relations Committee: political reconstruction, public order, border control, humanitarian problems, finding and securing WMD.

On January 15 the humanitarian groups that had been meeting at USAID asked for a meeting with Donald Rumsfeld or Paul Wolfowitz. They never got one. At an earlier meeting, according to a participant, they had been told, "The president has already spent an hour on the humanitarian issues." The most senior Pentagon official to meet with them was Joseph Collins, a deputy assistant secretary of defense. The representatives of the NGOs were generally the most senior and experienced figures from each organization; the government representatives were not of the same stature. "Without naming names, the people we met were not real decision-makers," Joel Charny says.

On January 24 a group of archaeologists and scholars went to the Pentagon to brief Collins and other officials about the most important historic sites in Iraq, so that they could be spared in bombing. Thanks to precision targeting, the sites would indeed survive combat. Many, of course, were pillaged almost immediately afterward.

On January 30 the International Rescue Committee, which had been participating in the weekly Iraq Working Group sessions, publicly warned that a breakdown of law and order was likely unless the victorious U.S. forces acted immediately, with martial law if necessary, to prevent it. A week later Refugees International issued a similar warning.

At the end of January, Sam Gardiner entered the picture. Gardiner is a retired air force colonel who taught for years at the National War College in Washington. His specialty is war gaming, and through the 1990s he was involved once or twice a year in major simulations involving an attack on Baghdad. In the late 1990s Gardiner had been a visiting scholar at the Swedish National Defense University, where he studied the effects of the bombing of Serbia's electrical grid. The big discovery was how long it took to get the system up and running again, after even a precise and limited attack. "Decapitation" attacks on a regime, like the one planned for Iraq, routinely begin with disabling the electrical grid. Gardiner warned that this Phase III step could cause big Phase IV problems.

Late in 2002 Gardiner had put together what he called a "net assessment" of how Iraq would look after a successful U.S. attack. His intended audience, in government, would recognize the designation as droll. "Net assessment" is a familiar term for a CIA-style intelligence analysis, but Gardiner also meant it to reflect the unusual origin of his data: none of it was classified, and all of it came from the Internet.

Through the power of search engines Gardiner was able to assemble what in other days would have seemed like a secret inside look at Iraq's infrastructure. He found electricity diagrams for the pumps used at Iraq's main water stations; he listed replacement parts for the most vulnerable elements of the electrical grid. He produced a scheme showing the elements of the system that would be easiest to attack but then quickest to repair. As it happened, damage to the electrical grid was a major postwar problem. Despite the precision of the bombing campaign, by mid-April wartime damage and immediate postwar looting had reduced Baghdad's power supply to one-fifth its prewar level, according to an internal Pentagon study. In mid-July the grid would be back to only half its prewar level, working on a three-hours-on, three-hours-off schedule.*

On January 19 Gardiner presented his net assessment, with information about Iraq's water, sewage, and public-health systems as well as its electrical grid, at an unclassified forum held by the RAND Corporation, in Washington. Two days later he presented it privately to Zalmay Khalilzad. Khalilzad was a former RAND analyst who had joined the Bush administration's National Security Council and before

---

*Along with the decline in public order, the failure to restore electric service was a major burden for civilians in postwar Iraq. According to the Brookings Institution's "Iraq Index," before the invasion, homes and businesses in Baghdad had electric power between 16 and 24 hours per day. By early 2006, Baghdad had power between 4 and 8 hours per day. The nationwide generating capacity had barely regained its prewar levels three years after the invasion.

the war was named the president's "special envoy and am-
bassador-at-large for Free Iraqis." (He has recently become
the U.S. ambassador to Afghanistan.*) Gardiner told me recently that Khalilzad was sobered by what he heard, and
gave Gardiner a list of other people in the government who
should certainly be shown the assessment. In the next few
weeks Gardiner presented his findings to Bear McConnell,
the USAID official in charge of foreign disaster relief, and
Michael Dunn, an air force general who had once been Gardiner's student and worked with the Joint Chiefs of Staff as
acting director for strategic plans and policy. A scheduled
briefing with Joseph Collins, who was becoming the Pentagon's point man for postwar planning, was canceled at the
last minute, after a description of Gardiner's report appeared in *Inside the Pentagon,* an influential newsletter.

The closer the nation came to war, the more the administration seemed to view people like Gardiner as virtual
Frenchmen—that is, softies who would always find some
excuse to oppose the war. In one sense they were right. "It
became clear that what I was really arguing was that we had
to delay the war," Gardiner told me. "I was saying, 'We
aren't ready, and in just six or eight weeks there is no way to
get ready for everything we need to do.'" (The first bombs
fell on Baghdad eight weeks after Gardiner's meeting with
Khalilzad.) "Everyone was very interested and very polite and

---

*Khalilzad, a native of Afghanistan, was U.S. Ambassador to that coun-
try from 2003 through the summer of 2005, when he succeeded John Negroponte as U.S. Ambassador to Iraq.

said I should talk to other people," Gardiner said. "But they had that 'Stalingrad stare'—people who had been doing stuff under pressure for too long and hadn't had enough sleep. You want to shake them and say, 'Are you really with me?'"

At the regular meeting of the Iraq Working Group on January 29, the NGO representatives discussed a recent piece of vital news. The administration had chosen a leader for all postwar efforts in Iraq: Jay M. Garner, a retired three-star army general who had worked successfully with the Kurds at the end of the Gulf War. The NGO representatives had no fault to find with the choice of Garner, but they were concerned, because his organization would be a subunit of the Pentagon rather than an independent operation or part of a civilian agency. "We had been pushing constantly to have reconstruction authority based in the State Department," Joel Charny told me. He and his colleagues were told by Wendy Chamberlin, a former ambassador to Pakistan who had become USAID's assistant administrator for the area including Iraq, that the NGOs should view Garner's appointment as a victory. After all, Garner was a civilian, and his office would draw representatives from across the government. "We said, 'C'mon, Wendy, his office is in the Pentagon!'" Charny says. Jim Bishop, a former U.S. ambassador who now works for InterAction, pointed out that the NGOs, like the U.S. government, were still hoping that other governments might help to fund humanitarian efforts. Bishop asked rhetorically, "Who from the international community is going to fund reconstruction run through the Pentagon?"

Garner assembled a team and immediately went to work. What happened to him in the next two months is the best-chronicled part of the postwar fiasco. He started from scratch, trying to familiarize himself with what the rest of the government had already done. On February 21 he convened a two-day meeting of diplomats, soldiers, academics, and development experts, who gathered at the National Defense University to discuss postwar plans. "The messiah could not have organized a sufficient relief and reconstruction or humanitarian effort in that short a time," a former CIA analyst named Judith Yaphe said after attending the meeting, according to Mark Fineman, Doyle McManus, and Robin Wright, of the *Los Angeles Times*. (Fineman died of a heart attack in fall 2003, while reporting from Baghdad.) Garner was also affected by tension between OSD and the rest of the government. Garner had heard about the Future of Iraq project, although Rumsfeld had told him not to waste his time reading it. Nonetheless, he decided to bring its director, Thomas Warrick, onto his planning team. Garner, who clearly does not intend to be the fall guy for postwar problems in Baghdad, told me last fall that Rumsfeld had asked him to kick Warrick off his staff. In an interview with the BBC last November, Garner confirmed details of the firing that had earlier been published in *Newsweek*. According to Garner, Rumsfeld asked him, " 'Jay, have you got a guy named Warrick on your team?' I said, 'Yes, I do.' He said, 'Well, I've got to ask you to remove him.' I said, 'I don't want to remove him; he's too valuable.' But he said, 'This came to me from such a high level that I can't overturn it, and I've just got to ask you to remove Mr. Warrick.'" *Newsweek*'s conclusion was that the man giving the instructions was Vice President Cheney.

This is the place to note that in several months of interviews I never once heard someone say "We took this step because the president indicated . . ." or "The president really wanted . . ." Instead I heard "Rumsfeld wanted," "Powell thought," "The vice president pushed," "Bremer asked," and so on. One need only compare this with any discussion of foreign policy in Reagan's or Clinton's administration— or Nixon's, or Kennedy's, or Johnson's, or most others—to sense how unusual is the absence of the president as prime mover. The other conspicuously absent figure was Condoleezza Rice, even after she was supposedly put in charge of coordinating administration policy on Iraq, in October 2003. It is possible that the president's confidants are so discreet that they have kept all his decisions and instructions secret. But that would run counter to the fundamental nature of bureaucratic Washington, where people cite a president's authority whenever they possibly can ("The president feels strongly about this, so . . .").*

To me, the more likely inference is that Bush took a

---

*The influences and positions of the administration's senior members will not, of course, be fully understood for years. But already it seems clear that decision-making Bush's major influence has been less intellectual than temperamental. When I wrote the paragraph above, late in 2003, it was true that few people I interviewed stressed the president's role in shaping the policy toward Iraq. But over the next two years, as the situation in Iraq became more difficult and the administration's policies became more controversial, I heard more and more frequent references to the president's "toughness" and "resolve" as important elements in determining American strategy. Specifically, as pressure rose late in 2005 for American withdrawal from Iraq, I often heard from military and civilian officials, "We'll be there as long as George Bush is in the White House."

strong overall position—fighting terrorism is this generation's challenge—and then was exposed to only a narrow
range of options worked out by the contending forces
within his administration. If this interpretation proves to be
right, and if Bush did in fact wish to know more, then blame
will fall on those whose responsibility it was to present him
with the widest range of choices: Cheney and Rice.

ONE MONTH BEFORE THE WAR

On February 14 Hans Blix reaffirmed to the United Nations
his view that Iraq had decided to cooperate with inspectors.
The division separating the United States and Britain from
France, Germany, and Russia became stark. On February 15
antiwar demonstrators massed in major cities around the
world: a million in Madrid, more than a million in Rome,
and a million or more in London, the largest demonstration
in Britain's history.

On February 21 Tony Blair joined George Bush at Camp
David, to underscore their joint determination to remove
the threat from Iraq.

THREE WEEKS BEFORE THE WAR

As the war drew near, the dispute about how to conduct it
became public. On February 25 the Senate Armed Services
Committee summoned all four Chiefs of Staff to answer questions about the war—and its aftermath. The crucial exchange

began with a question from the ranking Democrat, Carl Levin. He asked Eric Shinseki, the army chief of staff, how many soldiers would be required not to defeat Iraq but to occupy it. Well aware that he was at odds with his civilian superiors at the Pentagon, Shinseki at first deflected the question. "In specific numbers," he said, "I would have to rely on combatant commanders' exact requirements. But I think . . ." and he trailed off.

"How about a range?" Levin asked. Shinseki replied— and recapitulated the argument he had made to Rumsfeld.

"I would say that what's been mobilized to this point, something on the order of several hundred thousand soldiers, are probably, you know, a figure that would be required. We're talking about post-hostilities control over a piece of geography that's fairly significant, with the kinds of ethnic tensions that could lead to other problems. And so, it takes significant ground force presence to maintain safe and secure environment to ensure that the people are fed, that water is distributed, all the normal responsibilities that go along with administering a situation like this."

Two days later Paul Wolfowitz appeared before the House Budget Committee. He began working through his prepared statement about the Pentagon's budget request and then asked permission to "digress for a moment" and respond to recent commentary, "some of it quite outlandish, about what our postwar requirements might be in Iraq." Everyone knew he meant Shinseki's remarks.

"I am reluctant to try to predict anything about what the

cost of a possible conflict in Iraq would be," Wolfowitz said, "or what the possible cost of reconstructing and stabilizing that country afterward might be." This was more than reluctance—it was the administration's consistent policy before the war. "But some of the higher-end predictions that we have been hearing recently, such as the notion that it will take several hundred thousand U.S. troops to provide stability in post-Saddam Iraq, are wildly off the mark."

This was as direct a rebuke of a military leader by his civilian superior as the United States had seen in fifty years. Wolfowitz offered a variety of incidental reasons why his views were so different from those he alluded to: "I would expect that even countries like France will have a strong interest in assisting Iraq's reconstruction," and "We can't be sure that the Iraqi people will welcome us as liberators . . . [but] I am reasonably certain that they will greet us as liberators, and that will help us to keep requirements down." His fundamental point was this: "It's hard to conceive that it would take more forces to provide stability in post-Saddam Iraq than it would take to conduct the war itself and to secure the surrender of Saddam's security forces and his army. Hard to imagine."

None of the government working groups that had seriously looked into the question had simply "imagined" that occupying Iraq would be more difficult than defeating it. They had presented years' worth of experience suggesting that this would be the central reality of the undertaking. Wolfowitz either didn't notice this evidence or chose to disbelieve it. What David Halberstam said of Robert McNamara in *The Best and the Brightest* is true of those at OSD as well: they were brilliant, and they were fools.

TWO WEEKS BEFORE THE WAR

At the beginning of March, Andrew Natsios won a little-noticed but crucial battle. Because the United States had not yet officially decided whether to go to war, Natsios had not been able to persuade the Office of Management and Budget to set aside the money that USAID would need for immediate postwar efforts in Iraq. The battle was the more intense because Natsios, unlike his counterparts at the State Department, was both privately and publicly supportive of the case for war. Just before combat he was able to arrange an emergency $200 million grant from USAID to the World Food Programme. This money could be used to buy food immediately for Iraqi relief operations—and it helped to ensure that there were no postwar food shortages.

ONE WEEK BEFORE THE WAR

On March 13 humanitarian organizations had gathered at USAID headquarters for what was effectively the last meeting of the Iraq Working Group. Wendy Chamberlin, the senior USAID official present, discussed the impending war in terms that several participants noted, wrote down, and later mentioned to me. "It's going to be very quick," she said, referring to the actual war. "We're going to meet their immediate needs. We're going to turn it over to the Iraqis. And we're going to be out within the year."

On March 17 the United States, Britain, and Spain announced that they would abandon their attempt to get a second Security Council vote in favor of the war, and President Bush gave Saddam Hussein an ultimatum: leave the country within forty-eight hours or suffer the consequences. On March 19 the first bombs fell on Baghdad.

AFTERWARD

On April 9 U.S. forces took Baghdad. On April 14 the Pentagon announced that most of the fighting was over. On May 1 President Bush declared that combat operations were at an end. By then looting had gone on in Baghdad for several weeks. "When the United States entered Baghdad on April 9, it entered a city largely undamaged by a carefully executed military campaign," Peter Galbraith, a former U.S. ambassador to Croatia, told a congressional committee in June. "However, in the three weeks following the U.S. takeover, unchecked looting effectively gutted every important public institution in the city—with the notable exception of the oil ministry." On April 11, when asked why U.S. soldiers were not stopping the looting, Donald Rumsfeld said, "Freedom's untidy, and free people are free to make mistakes and commit crimes and do bad things. They're also free to live their lives and do wonderful things, and that's what's going to happen here."

This was a moment, as when he tore up the TPFDD, that Rumsfeld crossed a line. His embrace of "uncertainty" became a reckless evasion of responsibility. He had only disdain for "predictions," yes, and no one could have forecast every circumstance of postwar Baghdad. But virtually everyone who had thought about the issue had warned about the risk of looting. U.S. soldiers could have prevented it—and would have, if so instructed.

The looting spread, destroying the infrastructure that had survived the war and creating the expectation of future chaos. "There is this kind of magic moment, which you can't imagine until you see it," an American civilian who was in Baghdad during the looting told me. "People are used to someone being in charge, and when they realize no one is, the fabric rips."

On May 6 the administration announced that Bremer would be the new U.S. administrator in Iraq. Two weeks into that job Bremer disbanded the Iraqi army and other parts of the Baathist security structure.

If the failure to stop the looting was a major sin of omission, sending the Iraqi soldiers home was, in the view of nearly everyone except those who made the decision, a catastrophic error of commission. There were two arguments for taking this step. First, the army had "already disbanded itself," as Douglas Feith put it to me—soldiers had melted away, with their weapons. Second, the army had been an integral part of the Sunni-dominated Baathist security structure. Leaving it intact would be the wrong symbol for the new Iraq—especially for the Shiites, whom the army had oppressed. "These actions are part of a robust campaign to show the Iraqi people that the Saddam regime is gone, and will never return," a statement from Bremer's office said.

The case against wholesale dissolution of the army, rather

than a selective purge at the top, was that it created an instant enemy class: hundreds of thousands of men who still had their weapons but no longer had a paycheck or a place to go each day. Manpower that could have helped on security patrols became part of the security threat. Studies from the Army War College, the Future of Iraq project, and the Center for Strategic and International Studies, to name a few, had all considered exactly this problem and suggested ways of removing the noxious leadership while retaining the ordinary troops. They had all warned strongly against disbanding the Iraqi army. The Army War College, for example, said in its report, "To tear apart the army in the war's aftermath could lead to the destruction of one of the only forces for unity within the society."

"This is not something that was dreamed up by somebody at the last minute," Walter Slocombe—who held Feith's job, undersecretary of defense for policy, during the Clinton administration, and who is now a security adviser on Bremer's team—told Peter Slevin, of *The Washington Post*, November 2003. He said that he had discussed the plan with Wolfowitz at least once and with Feith several times, including the day before the order was given. "The critical point," he told Slevin, "was that nobody argued that we shouldn't do this." No one, that is, the administration listened to.*

---

*After this article was published, Slocombe wrote a letter to the editor of the *Atlantic*, complaining that I had not interviewed him directly about the disbanding of the Iraqi army. My rationalization was that Slocombe had been in Baghdad, and I in Washington, when I was researching the

Here is the hardest question: How could the administration have thought that it was safe to proceed in blithe indifference to the warnings of nearly everyone with operational experience in modern military occupations? Saying that the administration considered this a truly urgent "war of necessity" doesn't explain the indifference. Even if it feared that Iraq might give terrorists fearsome weapons at any moment, it could still have thought more carefully about the day after the war. World War II was a war of absolute necessity, and the United States still found time for detailed occupation planning.

The president must have known that however bright the scenarios, the reality of Iraq eighteen months after the war would affect his reelection. The political risk was enormous and obvious. Administration officials must have believed not only that the war was necessary but also that a successful occupation would not require any more forethought than they gave it.

It will be years before we fully understand how intelligent people convinced themselves of this. My guess is that three factors will be important parts of the explanation.

One is the panache of Donald Rumsfeld. He was near the zenith of his influence as the war was planned. His emphasis on the vagaries of life was all the more appealing within his

---

story—and moreover, since I had not singled him out as being responsible for the policy, I had a smaller obligation to hear his side of the story. But his point was fair. In 2005 I interviewed him at length on the same subject. The quotes from that interview appear on pages 159–161 of this book.

circle because of his jauntiness and verve. But he was not careful about remembering his practical obligations. Precisely because he could not foresee all hazards, he should have been more zealous about avoiding the ones that were evident—the big and obvious ones the rest of the government tried to point out to him.

A second is the triumphalism of the administration. In the twenty-five years since Ronald Reagan's rise, political conservatives have changed position in a way they have not fully recognized. Reagan's arrival marked the end of a half century of Democrat-dominated government in Washington. Yes, there has been one Democratic president since Reagan, and eventually there will be others. But as a rule the Republicans are now in command. Older Republicans—those who came of age in the 1960s and 1970s, those who are now in power in the administration—have not fully adjusted to this reality. They still feel like embattled insurgents, as if the liberals were in the driver's seat. They recognize their electoral strength but feel that in the battle of ideology their main task is to puncture fatuous liberal ideas.

The consequence is that Republicans are less used to exposing their own ideas to challenges than they should be. Today's liberals know there is a challenge to every aspect of their worldview. All they have to do is turn on the radio. Today's conservatives are more likely to think that any contrary ideas are leftovers from the tired 1960s, much as liberals of the Kennedy era thought that conservatives were in thrall to Herbert Hoover. In addition, the conservatives' understanding of modern history makes them think that their instincts are likely to be right and that their critics will be proved wrong. Europeans scorned Ronald Reagan, and the United Nations feared him, but in the end the Soviet Union was gone. So for reasons of personal, political, and intellectual history, it is understandable that members of this administration could proceed down one path in defiance of mounting evidence of its perils. The Democrats had similar destructive self-confidence in the 1960s, when they did their most grandiose Great Society thinking.

The third factor is the nature of the president himself. Leadership is always a balance between making large choices and being aware of details. George W. Bush has an obvious preference for large choices. This gave him his chance for greatness after the September 11 attacks. But his lack of curiosity about significant details may be his fatal weakness. When the decisions made during this time are assessed and judged, the administration will be found wanting for its carelessness. Because of warnings it chose to ignore, it squandered American prestige, fortune, and lives.

BUSH'S LOST YEAR

OCTOBER 2004

I remember distinctly the way 2002 began in Washington. New Year's Day was below freezing and blustery. The next day was worse. That day, January 2, I trudged several hundred yards across the vast parking lots of the Pentagon. I was being pulled apart by the wind and was ready to feel sorry for myself, until I was shamed by the sight of miserable, frozen army sentries at the numerous outdoor security posts that had been manned nonstop since the September 11 attacks.

I was going for an interview with Paul Wolfowitz, the deputy secretary of defense. At the time, Wolfowitz's name and face were not yet familiar worldwide. He was known in Washington for offering big-picture explanations of the administration's foreign-policy goals—a task for which the president was unsuited, the vice president was unavailable, and most other senior administration officials were, for various reasons, inappropriate. The national security adviser, Condoleezza Rice, was still playing a background role; the secretary of defense, Donald Rumsfeld, was mainly dealing with immediate operational questions in his daily briefings about the war in Afghanistan; the secretary of state, Colin Powell, was already known to be on the losing side of most internal policy struggles.

After the interview I wrote a short article about Wolfowitz and his views for the March 2002 issue of *The Atlantic Monthly*. In some ways the outlook and choices he described then still fit the world situation two and a half years later. Even at the time, the possibility that the administration's next move in the war on terror would be against Iraq, whether or not Iraq proved to be involved in the 9/11 hijackings, was under active discussion. When talking with me, Wolfowitz touched briefly on the case for removing Saddam Hussein, in the context of the general need to reduce tyranny in the Arab-Islamic world.*

But in most ways the assumptions and tone of the conver-

---

*Wolfowitz's argument, which I described in the March 2003, issue of *The Atlantic Monthly*, included a contrast between East Asian countries like the Philippines, Indonesia, and South Korea, which were slowly but unmistakably moving away from dictatorship, and Arab countries in the Middle East, which were not. "Success built on success" in East Asia, he said, as one country after another overthrew its tyrants—while in the Middle East, "you might say failure has built on failure." He continued:

Also, if you stop and think about the penalties for being known to favor any kind of positive political change in, say, Iraq, it's not surprising that there are a million Iraqis who favor positive political change—and they're all outside of Iraq. Inside, you don't survive.

The fact is that all the regimes that sponsor terrorism terrorize their own people . . . [Until now] there has been, not tolerance, but

sation now seem impossibly remote. At the beginning of 2002 the United States still operated in a climate of worldwide sympathy and solidarity. A broad range of allies supported its anti-Taliban efforts in Afghanistan, and virtually no international Muslim leaders had denounced them. President Bush was still being celebrated for his eloquent speech expressing American resolve, before a joint session of Congress on September 20. His deftness in managing domestic and international symbols was typified by his hosting an end-of-Ramadan ceremony at the White House in mid-December, even as battle raged in the Tora Bora region of Afghanistan, on the Pakistani border. At the start of 2002 fewer than 10,000 U.S. soldiers were deployed overseas as part of the war on terror, and a dozen Americans had died in combat. The United States had not captured Osama bin Laden, but it had routed the Taliban leadership that sheltered him, and it seemed to have put al-Qaeda on the run.

---

lack of intolerance toward support for terrorism. We had these 'terrorism lists,' and countries were put on them for supporting terrorism. It was a bad thing to do, but it wasn't considered *intolerable*. I think that after September 11 it's intolerable.

It seems to me that the political condition of the Muslim world and the Arab world was considered tolerable before. Not very nice, but you live with it. And I think that's not healthy—not healthy for us and certainly not healthy for them. Terrorists don't operate in a vacuum. They look at what happens to other terrorists. And hopefully now they are looking at what's happened in Afghanistan.

This logic, extended to Iraq, underscored the importance of overthrowing a tyrant and establishing a stable democracy there, so that other countries could learn from its example.

Because of the quick and, for Americans, nearly bloodless victory over the Taliban, the administration's national-security team had come to epitomize competence. During our talk Wolfowitz referred to "one reason this group of people work very well together," by which he meant that Cheney, Rumsfeld, Powell, and many others, including himself, had collaborated for years, from the Reagan administration through the 1991 Gulf War and afterward. From this experience they had developed a shared understanding of the nuances of "how to use force effectively," which they were now applying. In retrospect, the remarkable thing about Wolfowitz's comment was the assumption—which I then had no reason to challenge—that Bush's foreign-policy team was like a great business or sporting dynasty, which should be examined for secrets of success.

As I listen to the tape of that interview now, something else stands out: how expansive and unhurried even Wolfowitz sounded. "Even" Wolfowitz because since then he has become the symbol of an unrelenting drive toward war with Iraq. We now know that within the administration he was urging the case for "regime change" there immediately after 9/11. But when speaking for the record, more than a year before that war began, he stressed how broad a range of challenges the United States would have to address, and over how many years, if it wanted to contain the sources of terrorism. It would need to find ways to "lance the boil" of growing anti-Americanism, as it had done during the Reagan years by supporting democratic reform in South Korea and the Philippines. It would have to lead the Western world in celebrating and welcoming Turkey as the most successfully modernized Muslim country. It would need to understand that in the long run the most important part of America's policy was its moral example—that America stands for things "the rest of the world wants for itself."

I also remember the way 2002 ended. By late December some 200,000 members of the U.S. armed forces were en route to staging areas surrounding Iraq. Hundreds of thousands of people had turned out on the streets of London, Rome, Madrid, and other cities to protest the impending war. That it was impending was obvious, despite ongoing negotiations at the United Nations. Within weeks of the 9/11 attacks President Bush and Secretary Rumsfeld had asked to see plans for a possible invasion of Iraq. Congress voted to authorize the war in October. Immediately after the vote, planning bureaus inside the Pentagon were told to be ready for combat at any point between then and the following April. (Operation Iraqi Freedom actually began on March 19.) Declaring that it was impossible to make predictions about a war that might not occur, the administration refused to discuss plans for the war's aftermath—or its potential cost. In December the president fired Lawrence Lindsey, his chief economic adviser, after Lindsey offered a guess that the total cost might be $100 billion to $200 billion. As it happened, Lindsey's controversial estimate held up very well. By the summer of 2004, fifteen months after fighting began in Iraq, appropriations for war and occupation there totaled about $150 billion.* With more than 100,000 U.S.

---

*As discussed in the note on page 81 of this book, the long run costs may easily exceed $1 trillion.

soldiers still based in Iraq, the outlays will continue indefinitely at a rate of about $5 billion a month—much of it for fuel, ammunition, spare parts, and other operational needs. All this is at striking variance with the prewar insistence by Donald Rumsfeld and Paul Wolfowitz that Iraq's oil money, plus contributions from allies, would minimize the financial burden on Americans.

Despite the rout of al-Qaeda in Afghanistan, terror attacks, especially against Americans and Europeans, were rising at the end of 2002 and would continue to rise through 2003. Some 400 people worldwide had died in terror attacks in 2000, and some 300 in 2001, apart from the 3,000-plus killed on September 11. In 2002 more than 700 were killed, including 200 when a bomb exploded outside a Bali nightclub in October.

Whereas at the beginning of the year Paul Wolfowitz had sounded expansive about the many avenues the United States had to pursue in order to meet the terror threat, by the end of the year the focus was solely on Iraq, and the administration's tone was urgent. "Simply stated, there is no doubt that Saddam Hussein now has weapons of mass destruction," Vice President Cheney said in a major speech to the Veterans of Foreign Wars just before Labor Day. "There is no doubt he is amassing them to use against our friends, against our allies, and against us." Two weeks later, as Congress prepared for its vote to authorize the war, Condoleezza Rice said on CNN, "We do know that [Saddam Hussein] is actively pursuing a nuclear weapon ... We don't want the smoking gun to be a mushroom cloud."

On the last day of the year President Bush told reporters

at his ranch in Texas, "I hope this Iraq situation will be resolved peacefully. One of my New Year's resolutions is to work to deal with these situations in a way so that they're resolved peacefully." As he spoke, every operating branch of the government was preparing for war.

September 11, 2001, has so often been described as a "hinge event" that it is tempting to think no other events could rival its significance. Indeed, as a single shocking moment that changed Americans' previous assumptions, the only modern comparisons are Pearl Harbor and the assassination of John F. Kennedy. But as 9/11 enters history, it seems likely that the aftermath, especially the decisions made during 2002, will prove to be as significant as the attack itself. It is obviously too early to know the full historical effect of the Iraq campaign. The biggest question about post-Saddam Iraq—whether it is headed toward stability or toward new tyranny and chaos—may not be answered for years.

But the biggest question about the United States—whether its response to 9/11 has made it safer or more vulnerable—can begin to be answered. Over the past two years I have been talking with a group of people at the working level of America's antiterrorism efforts. Most are in the military, the intelligence agencies, and the diplomatic service; some are in think tanks and nongovernmental agencies. I have come to trust them, because most of them have no partisan ax to grind with the administration (in the nature of things, soldiers and spies are mainly Republicans), and because they have so far been proved right. In the year before combat started in Iraq, they warned that occupying the country would be far harder than conquering it. As the occupation began, they pointed out the existence of plans and warnings the administration seemed determined to ignore.

As a political matter, whether the United States is now safer or more vulnerable is of course ferociously controversial. That the war was necessary—and beneficial—is the Bush administration's central claim. That it was not is the central claim of its critics. But among national-security professionals there is surprisingly little controversy. Except for those in government and in the opinion industries whose job it is to defend the administration's record, they tend to see America's response to 9/11 as a catastrophe. I have sat through arguments among soldiers and scholars about whether the invasion of Iraq should be considered the worst strategic error in American history—or only the worst since Vietnam. Some of these people argue that the United States had no choice but to fight, given a prewar consensus among its intelligence agencies that Iraq actually had WMD supplies. Many say that things in Iraq will eventually look much better than they do now. But about the conduct and effect of the war in Iraq one view prevails: it has increased the threats America faces, and has reduced the military, financial, and diplomatic tools with which we can respond.

"Let me tell you my gut feeling," a senior figure at one of America's military-sponsored think tanks told me recently, after we had talked for twenty minutes about details of the campaigns in Afghanistan and Iraq. "If I can be blunt, the administration is full of shit. In my view we are much, much worse off now than when we went into Iraq. That is not a partisan position. I voted for these guys. But I think they are incompetent, and I have had a very close perspective on what is happening. Certainly in the long run we have harmed ourselves. We are playing to the enemy's political advantage. Whatever tactical victories we may gain along the way, this will prove to be a strategic blunder."

This man will not let me use his name, because he is still involved in military policy. He cited the experiences of Joseph Wilson, Richard Clarke, and Generals Eric Shinseki and Anthony Zinni to illustrate the personal risks of openly expressing his dissenting view. But I am quoting him anonymously—as I will quote some others—because his words are representative of what one hears at the working level.

To a surprising extent their indictment doesn't concentrate on the aspect of the problem most often discussed in public: exactly why the United States got the WMD threat so wrong. Nor does it involve the problem previously discussed in *The Atlantic Monthly* (and in the second chapter of this book): the administration's failure, whether deliberate or inadvertent, to make use of the careful and extensive planning for postwar Iraq that had been carried out by the State Department, the CIA, various branches of the military, and many other organizations. Rather, these professionals argue that by the end of 2002 the decisions the administration had made—and avoided making—through the course of the year had left the nation less safe, with fewer positive options. Step-by-step through 2002 America's war on terror became little more than its preparation for war in Iraq.

Because of that shift, the United States succeeded in removing Saddam Hussein, but at this cost: The first front in the war on terror, Afghanistan, was left to fester, as attention and money were drained toward Iraq. This in turn left more havens in Afghanistan in which terrorist groups could reconstitute themselves; a resurgent opium-poppy economy to finance them; and more of the disorder and brutality the United States had hoped to eliminate. Whether or not the strong international alliance that began the assault on the Taliban might have brought real order to Afghanistan is impossible to say. It never had the chance, because America's premature withdrawal soon fractured the alliance and curtailed postwar reconstruction. Indeed, the campaign in Afghanistan was warped and limited from the start, by a preexisting desire to save troops for Iraq.

A full inventory of the costs of war in Iraq goes on. President Bush began 2002 with a warning that North Korea and Iran, not just Iraq, threatened the world because of the nuclear weapons they were developing. With the United States preoccupied by Iraq, these other two countries surged ahead. They have been playing a game of chess, or nerves, against America—and if they have not exactly won, they have advanced by several moves. Because it lost time and squandered resources, the United States now has no good options for dealing with either country. It has fewer deployable soldiers and weapons; it has less international leverage through the "soft power" of its alliances and treaties; it even has worse intelligence, because so many resources are directed toward Iraq.

At the beginning of 2002 the United States imported over 50 percent of its oil. In two years we have increased that figure by nearly 10 percent. The need for imported oil is the fundamental reason the United States must be deferential in its relationship with Saudi Arabia. Revenue from that oil is the fundamental reason that extremist groups based in Saudi Arabia were so rich. After the first oil shocks, in the mid-1970s, the United States took steps that reduced its imports of Persian Gulf oil. The Bush administration could have made similar steps a basic part of its antiterrorism strategy, and could have counted on making progress: through most of 2002 the administration could assume bipartisan support for nearly anything it proposed. But its only such suggestion was drilling in the Arctic National Wildlife Refuge.

Before America went to war in Iraq, its military power seemed limitless. There was less need to actually apply it when all adversaries knew that anytime we did so we would win. Now the limits on our military's manpower and sustainability are all too obvious. For example, the administration announced this summer that in order to maintain troop levels in Iraq, it would withdraw 12,500 soldiers from South Korea. The North Koreans, the Chinese, the Iranians, the Syrians, and others who have always needed to take into account the chance of U.S. military intervention now realize that America has no stomach for additional wars. Before Iraq the U.S. military was turning away qualified applicants. Now it applies "stop-loss" policies that forbid retirement or resignation by volunteers, and it has mobilized the National Guard and Reserves in a way not seen since World War II.

Because of outlays for Iraq, the United States cannot spend $150 billion for other defensive purposes. Some nine million shipping containers enter American ports each year;

only 2 percent of them are physically inspected, because inspecting more would be too expensive. The Department of Homeland Security, created after 9/11, is a vast grab bag of federal agencies, from the Coast Guard to the Border Patrol to the former Immigration and Naturalization Service; ongoing operations in Iraq cost significantly more each month than all Homeland Security expenses combined. The department has sought to help cities large and small to improve their "first responder" systems, especially with better communications for their fire and emergency medical services. This summer a survey by the U.S. Conference of Mayors found that fewer than a quarter of 231 major cities under review had received any of the aid they expected. An internal budget memo from the administration was leaked this past spring. It said that outlays for virtually all domestic programs, including homeland security, would have to be cut in 2005—and the federal budget deficit would still be more than $450 billion.

Worst of all, the government-wide effort to wage war in Iraq crowded out efforts to design a broader strategy against Islamic extremists and terrorists; to this day the administration has articulated no comprehensive long-term plan. It dismissed out of hand any connection between policies toward the Israeli–Palestinian conflict and increasing tension with many Islamic states. Regime change in Iraq, it said, would have a sweeping symbolic effect on worldwide sources of terror. That seems to have been true—but in the opposite way from what the president intended. It is hard to find a counterterrorism specialist who thinks that the Iraq

War has reduced rather than increased the threat to the United States.

And here is the startling part. There is no evidence that the president and those closest to him ever talked systematically about the "opportunity costs" and trade-offs in their decision to invade Iraq. No one has pointed to a meeting, a memo, a full set of discussions, about what America would gain and lose.

THE PRELUDE: LATE 2001

Success in war requires an understanding of who the enemy is, what resources can be used against him, and how victory will be defined. In the immediate aftermath of 9/11 America's expert agencies concluded that Osama bin Laden and al-Qaeda were almost certainly responsible for the attacks—and that the Taliban regime in Afghanistan was providing them with sanctuary. Within the government there was almost no dispute, then or later, about the legitimacy and importance of destroying that stronghold. Indeed, the main criticism of the initial anti-Taliban campaign was that it took so long to start.

In his book *Against All Enemies* the former terrorism adviser Richard Clarke says it was "plainly obvious" after September 11 that "al Qaeda's sanctuary in Taliban-run Afghanistan had to be occupied by U.S. forces and the al Qaeda leaders killed." It was therefore unfortunate that the move against the Taliban was "slow and small." Soon after the attacks President Bush created an interagency Campaign Coordination Committee to devise responses to al-Qaeda, and named Clarke its cochairman. Clarke told me that this group urged a "rapid, no-holds-barred" retaliation in Afghanistan—including an immediate dispatch of troops to Afghanistan's borders to cut off al-Qaeda escape routes.

But the administration was unwilling to use overwhelming power in Afghanistan. The only authorized account of how the "principals"—the big shots of the administration—felt and thought at this time is in Bob Woodward's books *Bush at War* (2002) and *Plan of Attack* (2004), both based on interviews with the president and his senior advisers. To judge by *Bush at War,* Woodward's more laudatory account, a major reason for delay in attacking the Taliban had to do with "CSAR"—combat search and rescue teams. These were meant to be in place before the first aerial missions, so that they could go to the aid of any American pilot who might be downed. Preparations took weeks. They involved negotiations with the governments of Tajikistan and Uzbekistan for basing rights, the slow process of creating and equipping support airstrips in remote mountainous regions, and the redeployment of far-flung aircraft carriers to the Persian Gulf.

"The slowness was in part because the military weren't ready and they needed to move in the logistics support, the refueling aircraft, all of that," Richard Clarke told me. "But through this time the president kept saying to the Taliban, 'You still have an opportunity to come clean with us.' Which I thought—and the State Department thought—was silly. We'd already told them in advance that if this hap-

pened we were going to hold them personally responsible."
Laurence Pope, a former ambassador to Chad, made a similar point when I spoke with him. Through the late 1990s
Pope was the political adviser to General Zinni, who as the
head of U.S. Central Command was responsible for Iraq
and Afghanistan. Pope had run war games concerning assaults on both countries. "We had warned the Taliban repeatedly about Osama bin Laden," he told me, referring to
the late Clinton years. "There was no question [after 9/11]
that we had to take them on and deny that sanctuary to al-
Qaeda. We should have focused like a laser on bin Laden
and taking down al-Qaeda, breaking crockery in the neigh-
borhood if necessary."

The crockery he was referring to included the government of Pakistan, which viewed the Pashtun tribal areas
along the Afghan border as ungovernable. In the view of
Pope and some others, the United States should have insisted on going into these areas right away, either with Pakistani troops or on its own—equipped with money to buy
support, weapons, or both. This might have caused some regional and international disruption—but less than later invading Iraq.

It was on October 6, three and a half weeks after the attacks, that President Bush issued his final warning that
"time was running out" for the Taliban to turn over bin
Laden. The first cruise-missile strikes occurred the next day.
The first paramilitary teams from the CIA and Special Forces
arrived shortly thereafter; the first regular U.S. combat troops
were deployed in late November. Thus, while the United
States prepared for its response, Osama bin Laden, his deputy

Ayman al-Zawahiri, and the rest of their ruling Shura Council had almost two months to flee and hide.

Opinions vary about exactly how much difference it would have made if the United States had killed or captured al-Qaeda's leaders while the World Trade Center ruins were still smoldering. But no one disputes that the United States needed to move immediately against al-Qaeda, and in the most complete and decisive way possible. And there is little disagreement about what happened next. The military and diplomatic effort in Afghanistan was handicapped from the start because the administration had other concerns, and it ended badly even though it started well.

WINTER 2001–2002: WAR ON THE CHEAP

By the beginning of 2002 U.S. and Northern Alliance forces had beaten the Taliban but lost bin Laden. At that point the United States faced a consequential choice: to bear down even harder in Afghanistan, or to shift the emphasis in the global war on terror (GWOT, as it is known in the trade) somewhere else.

A version of this choice between Afghanistan and "some-where else" had in fact been made at the very start of the ad-ministration's response to the 9/11 attacks. As Clarke, Woodward, and others have reported, during the top-level meetings at Camp David immediately after the attacks Paul Wolfowitz forcefully argued that Saddam Hussein was so threatening, and his overthrow was so "doable," that he had to be included in the initial military response. "The 'Afghanistan first' argument prevailed, basically for the reasons that Colin Powell advocated," Richard Clarke told me. "He said that the American people just aren't going to understand if you don't do something in Afghanistan right away—and that the lack of causal connection between Iraq and 9/11 would make it difficult to make the case for that war."

But Afghanistan first did not mean Afghanistan only. Clarke reminded me that he had prepared a memo on antiterrorism strategy for the president's review before September 11. When it came back, on September 17, Clarke noticed only one significant change: the addition of a paragraph asking the Defense Department to prepare war plans for Iraq. Throughout the fall and winter, as U.S. troops were deployed in Afghanistan, Bush asked for and received increasingly detailed briefings from General Tommy Franks about the forces that might later be necessary in Iraq. According to many people who observed the process, the stated and unstated need to be ready for Saddam Hussein put a serious crimp in the U.S. effort against bin Laden and the Taliban.

The need to reserve troops for a likely second front in Iraq was one factor, though not the only one, in the design of the U.S. battle plan for Afghanistan. Many in the press (including me) marveled at America's rapid move against the Taliban for the ingenuity of its tactics. Instead of sending in many thousands of soldiers, the administration left much of the actual fighting to the tribes of the Northern Alliance. Although the U.S. forces proved unable to go in fast, they certainly went in light—the Special Forces soldiers who chose targets for circling B-52s while picking their way through mountains on horseback being the most famous example. And they very quickly won. All this was exactly in keeping with the "transformation" doctrine that Donald Rumsfeld had been emphasizing in the Pentagon, and it reflected Rumsfeld's determination to show that a transformed military could substitute precision, technology, and imagination for sheer manpower.

But as would later become so obvious in Iraq, ousting a regime is one thing, and controlling or even pacifying a country is something else. For a significant group of military and diplomatic officials within the U.S. government, winning this "second war," for postcombat stability in Afghanistan, was a crucial step in the administration's long-term efforts against al-Qaeda. Afghanistan had, after all, been the site of al-Qaeda's main training camps. The Taliban who harbored al-Qaeda had originally come to power as an alternative to warlordism and an economy based on extortion and drugs, so the United States could ill afford to let the country revert to the same rule and economy.

In removing the Taliban, the United States had acted as a genuine liberator. It came to the task with clean hands and broad international support. It had learned from the Soviet Union the folly of trying to hold Afghanistan by force. But it did not have to control the entire country to show that U.S. intervention could have lasting positive effects. What it needed, according to the "second war" group, was a sustained military, financial, and diplomatic effort to keep

Afghanistan from sinking back toward chaos and thus becoming a terrorist haven once again.

"Had we seen Afghanistan as anything other than a sideshow," says Larry Goodson, a scholar at the Army War College who spent much of 2002 in Afghanistan, "we could have stepped up both the economic and security presence much more quickly than we did. Had Iraq not been what we were ginning up for in 2002, when the security situation in Afghanistan was collapsing, we might have come much more quickly to the peacekeeping and 'nation-building' strategy we're beginning to employ now." Iraq, of course, was what we were ginning up for, and the effects on Afghanistan were more important, if subtler, than has generally been discussed.

I asked officials, soldiers, and spies whether they had witnessed trade-offs—specific transfers of manpower—that materially affected U.S. success in Afghanistan, and the response of Thomas White was typical: not really. During the wars in Afghanistan and Iraq, White was secretary of the army. Like most other people I spoke with, he offered an example or two of Iraq-Afghanistan trade-offs, mainly involving strain on Special Forces or limits on electronic intelligence from the National Security Agency (NSA). Another man told me that NSA satellites had to be "boreholed" in a different direction—that is, aimed directly at sites in Iraq, rather than at Afghanistan. But no one said that changes like these had really been decisive. What did matter, according to White and nearly everyone else I spoke with, was the knowledge that the "center of gravity" of the antiterrorism campaign was about to shift to Iraq. That dictated not just the vaunted "lightness" of the invasion but also the decision to designate allies for crucial tasks: the Northern Alliance for initial combat, and the Pakistanis for closing the border so that al-Qaeda leaders would not escape. In the end neither ally performed its duty the way the Americans had hoped. The Northern Alliance was far more motivated to seize Kabul than to hunt for bin Laden. The Pakistanis barely pretended to patrol the border. In its recent "after-action reports" the U.S. military has been increasingly critical of its own management of this campaign, but delegating the real work to less motivated allies seems to have been the uncorrectable error.

The desire to limit U.S. commitment had at least as great an effect on what happened after the fall of the Taliban. James Dobbins, who was the Bush administration's special envoy for Afghanistan and its first representative in liberated Kabul, told me that three decisions in the early months "really shaped" the outcome in Afghanistan. "One was that U.S. forces were not going to do peacekeeping of any sort, under any circumstances. They would remain available to hunt down Osama bin Laden and find renegade Taliban, but they were not going to have any role in providing security for the country at large. The second was that we would oppose anybody else's playing this role outside Kabul. And this was at a time when there was a good deal of interest from other countries in doing so." A significant reason for refusing help, according to Dobbins, was that accepting it would inevitably have tied up more American resources in

Afghanistan, especially for airlifting donated supplies to foreign-led peacekeeping stations in the hinterland. The third decision was that U.S. forces would not engage in any counternarcotics activities. One effect these policies had was to prolong the disorder in Afghanistan and increase the odds against a stable government. The absence of American or international peacekeepers guaranteed that the writ of the new Karzai government would extend, at best, to Kabul itself.

"I can't prove this, but I believe they didn't want to put in a lot of regular infantry because they wanted to hold it in reserve," Richard Clarke explains. "And the issue is the infantry. A rational military planner who was told to stabilize Afghanistan after the Taliban was gone, and who was not told that we might soon be doing Iraq, would probably have put in three times the number of infantry, plus all the logistics support 'tail.' He would have put in more civil-affairs units, too. Based on everything I heard at the time, I believe I can make a good guess that the plan for Afghanistan was affected by a predisposition to go into Iraq. The result of that is that they didn't have enough people to go in and stabilize the country, nor enough people to make sure these guys didn't get out."

The administration later placed great emphasis on making Iraq a showcase of Islamic progress: a society that, once freed from tyranny, would demonstrate steady advancement toward civil order, economic improvement, and, ultimately, democracy. Although Afghanistan is a far wilder, poorer country, it might have provided a better showcase, and sooner. There was no controversy about America's involvement; the rest of the world was ready to provide aid; if it wasn't going to become rich, it could become demonstrably less poor. The amount of money and manpower sufficient to transform Afghanistan would have been a tiny fraction of what America decided to commit in Iraq. But the opportunity was missed, and Afghanistan began a descent to its pre-Taliban warlord state.

SPRING 2002: CHAOS AND CLOSED MINDS

Early 2002 was the administration's first chance to look beyond its initial retaliation in Afghanistan. This could have been a time to think broadly about America's vulnerabilities and to ask what problems might have been overlooked in the immediate response to 9/11. At this point the United States still had comfortable reserves of all elements of international power, "hard" and "soft" alike.

As the fighting wound down in Tora Bora, the administration could in principle have matched a list of serious problems with a list of possible solutions. In his State of the Union speech, in late January, President Bush had named Iran, Iraq, and North Korea as an "axis of evil." The administration might have weighed the relative urgency of those three threats, including uncontested evidence that North Korea was furthest along in developing nuclear weapons. It might have launched an all-out effort to understand al-Qaeda's strengths and weaknesses—and to exploit the weak points. It might have asked whether relations with Pakistan,

Egypt, and Saudi Arabia needed fundamental reconsideration. For decades we had struck an inglorious bargain with the regimes in those countries: we would overlook their internal repression and their role as havens for Islamic extremists; they would not oppose us on first-order foreign-policy issues—demonstrating, for instance, a relative moderation toward Israel. And the Saudis would be cooperative about providing oil. Maybe, after serious examination, this bargain would still seem to be the right one, despite the newly manifest dangers of Islamic extremism. But the time to ask the question was early in 2002.

The administration might also have asked whether its approach to Israel and the Palestinians needed reconsideration. Before 9/11 it had declared a hands-off policy toward Israel and the PLO, but sooner or later all Bush's predecessors had come around to a "land for peace" bargain as the only plausible solution in the Middle East. The new administration would never have more leverage or a more opportune moment for imposing such a deal than soon after it was attacked.

Conceivably the administration could have asked other questions—about energy policy, about manpower in the military, about the fiscal base for a sustained war. This was an opportunity created by crisis. At the top level of the administration attention swung fast, and with little discussion, exclusively to Iraq. This sent a signal to the working levels, where daily routines increasingly gave way to preparations for war, steadily denuding the organizations that might have been thinking about other challenges.

The administration apparently did not consider questions like "If we pursue the war on terror by invading Iraq, might we incite even more terror in the long run?" and "If we commit so many of our troops this way, what possibilities will we be giving up?" But Bush "did not think of this, intellectually, as a comparative decision," I was told by Senator Bob Graham, of Florida, who voted against the war resolution for fear it would hurt the fight against terrorism. "It was a single decision: he saw Saddam Hussein as an evil person who had to be removed."* The firsthand accounts of the administration's decision-making indicate that the president spent most of his time looking at evidence of Saddam Hussein's threat, and significant but smaller amounts of time trying to build his coalition and hearing about the invasion plans. A man who participated in high-level planning for both Afghanistan and Iraq—and who is unnamed here because he still works for the government—told me, "There was absolutely no debate in the normal sense. There are only six or eight of them who make the decisions, and they only talk to each other. And if you disagree with them in public, they'll come after you, the way they did with Shinseki."

The three known exceptions to this pattern actually underscore the limits on top-level talks. One was the discussions at Camp David just after 9/11: they led to "Afghanistan

---

*A year and a half after this article was written, there are still virtually no cases of President Bush or Vice President Cheney publicly discussing the war in Iraq in a comparative sense. That is, they do not weigh it against other threats to American security so as to measure the costs and benefits of the decision to invade. Instead, they still present it as what Senator Graham called a "single decision": that Saddam Hussein had to go.

first," which delayed rather than forestalled the concentration on Iraq. The second was Colin Powell's "You break it, you've bought it" warning to the president in the summer of 2002: far from leading to serious questions about the war, it did not even persuade the administration to use the postwar plans devised by the State Department, the army, and the CIA. The third was a long memo from Rumsfeld to Bush a few months before the war began, when a campaign against Iraq was a foregone conclusion. As excerpted in *Plan of Attack,* it listed twenty-nine ways in which an invasion could backfire. "Iraq could successfully best the U.S. in public relations and persuade the world that it was a war against Muslims" was one. "There could be higher than expected collateral damage" was another. But even this memo was couched in terms of "making sure that we had done everything humanly possible to prepare [the president] for what could go wrong, to prepare so things would go right," Rumsfeld explained to Bob Woodward. And its only apparent effect was that Bush called in his military commanders to look at the war plans.

Discussions at the top were distorted in yet another way—by an unspoken effect of disagreements over the Middle East. Some connections between Iraq policy and the Israeli-Palestinian dispute are obvious. One prowar argument was "The road to Jerusalem runs through Baghdad"— that is, once the United States had removed Saddam Hussein and the threat he posed to Israel, it could lean more effectively on Ariel Sharon and the Likud government to accept the right deal. According to this logic, America could also

lean more effectively on the Palestinians and their supporters, because of the new strength it would have demonstrated
by liberating Iraq. The contrary argument—"The road to
Baghdad leads through Jerusalem"—appears to have been
raised mainly by Tony Blair. Its point was that if the United
States first took a tougher line with Sharon and recognized
that the Palestinians, too, had grievances, it would have a
much easier time getting allied support and Arab acquiescence for removing Saddam Hussein. There is no evidence
that this was ever significantly discussed inside the administration.

"The groups on either side of the Iraq debate basically
didn't trust each other," a former senior official in the administration told me—and the people "on either side" he
was speaking of all worked for George Bush. (He, too, insisted on anonymity because he has ongoing dealings with
the government.) "If it wasn't clear why you were saying
these skeptical things about invading Iraq, there was naturally the suspicion that you were saying [them] because you
opposed the Israeli position. So any argument became suspect." Suspicion ran just as strongly the other way—that officials were steadfast for war because they supported the
Israeli position. In this (admittedly oversimplified) schema,
the CIA, the State Department, and the uniformed military
were the most skeptical of war—and, in the view of war
supporters, were also the most critical of Israel. The White
House (Bush, Cheney, Rice) and the Defense Department's
civilian leadership were the most prowar—and the most
pro-Israel. Objectively, all these people agreed far more than

they differed, but their mutual suspicions further muted dissenting views.

At the next level down, different problems had the same effect: difficulty in thinking broadly about threats and responses. An obscure-sounding bureaucratic change contributed. At the start of his second term Bill Clinton had signed PDD 56, a presidential decision directive about handling international emergencies. The idea was that, like it or not, a chaotic world would continually involve the United States in "complex contingency operations." These were efforts, like the ones in the Balkans and East Africa, in which soldiers, diplomats, relief workers, reconstruction experts, economists, legal authorities, and many other officials from many different institutions would need to work together if any of them were to succeed. The directive set up a system for coordinating these campaigns, so that no one organization dominated the others or operated unilaterally.

When it took office, the Bush administration revoked this plan and began working on a replacement. But nothing was on hand as of September 11. For months the response to the attacks was managed by a variety of ad hoc groups. The Campaign Coordination Committee, run by Richard Clarke and his colleague Franklin Miller, oversaw strategies against al-Qaeda. The new Domestic Preparedness Committee, run by John Ashcroft's deputy, Larry Thompson, oversaw internal security measures. And the "principals"—Bush, Cheney, Rumsfeld, Powell, Rice, Director of Central Intelligence George Tenet, and a few others, including Wolfowitz, Powell's deputy Richard Armitage, and Cheney's aide Lewis

"Scooter" Libby—met frequently to plan the showdown with Iraq. There was no established way to make sure that State knew what Defense was doing and vice versa, as became disastrously obvious after the fall of Baghdad. And there was no recognized venue for opportunity-cost discussions about the emerging Iraq policy, even if anyone had wanted them.

In the absence of other plans, initiative on every issue was increasingly taken in the Pentagon. And within the Pentagon the emphasis increasingly moved toward Iraq. In March 2002, when U.S. troops were still engaged in Operation Anaconda on the Afghan–Pakistani border, and combat in Iraq was still a year away, inside the government Afghanistan had begun to seem like yesterday's problem. When asked about Iraq at a press conference on March 13, Bush said merely, "All options are on the table." By that time Tommy Franks had answered Bush's request for battle plans and lists of potential bombing targets in Iraq.

The more experienced in government the people I interviewed were, the more likely they were to stress the importance of the mental shift in the spring of 2002. When I asked Richard Clarke whether preparations for Iraq had really taken anything crucial from Afghanistan or other efforts, he said yes, unquestionably. "They took one thing that people on the outside find hard to believe or appreciate," he said. "Management time. We're a huge government, and we have hundreds of thousands of people involved in national security. Therefore you would think we could walk and chew gum at the same time. I've never found that to be true.

You've got one national security adviser and one CIA director, and they each have one deputy. The same is true in Defense. Interestingly in terms of the military, both of these wars took place in the same 'CINCdom' "—by which Clarke meant that both were in the realm of Tommy Franks's Central Command, rather than in two different theaters. "It just is not credible that the principals and the deputies paid as much attention to Afghanistan or the war against al-Qaeda as they should have."

According to Michael Scheuer, a career CIA officer who spent the late 1990s as head of the agency's anti–bin Laden team, the shift of attention had another destructive effect on efforts to battle al-Qaeda: the diversion of members of that team and the agency's limited supply of Arabic speakers and Middle East specialists to support the mounting demand for intelligence on Iraq. (Because Scheuer is still on active duty at the CIA, the agency allowed him to publish his recent book, *Imperial Hubris,* a harsh criticism of U.S. approaches to controlling terrorism, only as "Anonymous." After we spoke, his identity was disclosed by Jason Vest, in the Boston *Phoenix;* when I met him, he declined to give his name and was introduced simply as "Mike."*) "With a finite number of people who have any kind of pertinent experience," Scheuer told me, "there is unquestionably a sucking away of resources from Afghanistan and al-Qaeda to Iraq, just because it was a much bigger effort."

---

*Shortly after this article appeared, Scheuer resigned from the CIA and began giving interviews and speeches under his own name.

Scheuer observed that George Tenet had claimed early in 2003 that there was enough expertise and manpower to handle both Iraq and al-Qaeda. "From inside the system that sounded like a very questionable judgment," Scheuer said. "You start with a large group of people who have worked bin Laden and al-Qaeda and Sunni terrorism for years—and worked it every day since 9/11. Then you move a lot of people out to work the Iraq issue, and instead you have a lot of people who come in for ninety days or one hundred and twenty days, then leave. It's like any other profession. Over time you make connections. A name comes up, and there's nothing on file in the last two years—but you remember that five years ago there was a guy with that name doing acts in the Philippines. If you don't have an institutional memory, you don't make the connection. When they talk about connecting the dots, the computers are important. But at the end of the day, the most important thing is that human being who's been working this issue for five or six years. You can have the best computers in the world, and you can have an ocean of information, but if you have a guy who's only been there for three weeks or three months, you're very weak."

Laurence Pope, the former ambassador, told me that Iraq monomania was particularly destructive in the spring of 2002 because of the opportunity that came and went in Afghanistan. "There was a moment of six months or so when we could have put much more pressure on the tribal areas [to get al-Qaeda], and on Pakistan, and done a better job of reconstruction in Afghanistan," he said. "In reality, the Beltway can only do one thing at a time, and because of the attention to Iraq, what should have happened in Afghanistan didn't."

So by the spring, after six months in which to consider its strategy, the administration had radically narrowed its choices. Its expert staffers were deflected toward Iraq—and away from Afghanistan, Iran, North Korea, Israel-Palestine, the hunt for bin Laden, the assault on al-Qaeda, even China and Taiwan. Its diplomats were not squeezing Pakistan as hard as possible about chasing al-Qaeda, or Saudi Arabia about cracking down on extremists, because the United States needed their help—or at least acquiescence—in the coming war with Iraq. Its most senior officials were working out the operational details of a plan whose fundamental wisdom they had seldom, if ever, stopped to examine.

SUMMER AND FALL: THE ONE-FRONT WAR

President Bush's first major statement about his post-9/11 foreign policy had come in his State of the Union address. His second came on June 1, when he gave the graduation speech at West Point. It carefully laid out the case for a new doctrine of "preemptive" war. Bush didn't say "Iraq" or "Saddam Hussein," but his meaning was unmistakable. "Containment is not possible when unbalanced dictators with weapons of mass destruction can deliver those weapons on missiles or secretly provide them to terrorist allies," he said. "We cannot put our faith in the word of tyrants who solemnly sign non-proliferation treaties and then systemically break them. If we wait for threats to fully materialize, we will have waited too long." A few weeks later Condoleezza Rice presented a fuller version of the concept, and Dick Cheney hammered home his warnings that Saddam Hussein had, beyond all doubt, acquired weapons of mass destruction. In September, Donald Rumsfeld said at a news conference that the link between Saddam Hussein and al-Qaeda was "not debatable." By October, Bush had practically stopped referring to Osama bin Laden in his press statements; he said of Saddam Hussein, "This is the guy that tried to kill my dad."

The Democrats still controlled the Senate, but on October 11 Majority Leader Tom Daschle led John Kerry, John Edwards, and twenty-six other Democrats in voting to authorize the war. (Authorization passed the Senate 77–23; most Democrats in the House voted against it, but it still carried there, by 296 to 133.) Democratic officials were desperate to get the vote behind them, so that in the impending midterm elections they could not be blamed for hampering the war on terrorism—in which, the administration said, war in Iraq played an integral part.

The Cyclops-like nature of the administration's perception of risk became more evident. Uncertain evidence about Iraq was read in the most pessimistic fashion; much more reliable evidence about other threats was ignored. Of the three members of the "axis of evil," Iraq had made the sketchiest progress toward developing nuclear weapons. In October, just before the Iraq War vote, a delegation of Americans in Pyongyang found that North Korea's nuclear-weapons program was actually up and running. As the weeks wore on, North Korea became more and more brazen. In December it reactivated a nuclear processing plant it had closed eight years earlier as part of a deal with the United States. Soon thereafter it kicked out inspectors from the International Atomic Energy Agency and announced that it would withdraw from the Nuclear Non-Proliferation Treaty. North Korea was dropping even the pretense that it was not developing nuclear bombs.

Meanwhile, in August 2002, an Iranian opposition group revealed the existence of two previously secret nuclear facilities, in Natanz and Arak. The first was devoted to uranium enrichment, the second to heavy-water production, which is a step toward producing plutonium. Months before the vote on war with Iraq, then, the United States had very strong indications that Iran was pursuing two paths toward atomic weaponry: uranium and plutonium. The indications from North Korea were at least as strong. If the very worst prewar suspicions about Saddam Hussein's weapons of mass destruction had turned out to be true, the nuclear stakes would still have been lower than those in North Korea or Iran.

"How will history judge this period, in terms of the opportunity costs of invading Iraq?" said John Pike, the director of GlobalSecurity.org, when we spoke. "I think the opportunity cost is going to be North Korea and Iran. I mean, in 2002 it became obvious that Iran has a full-blown nuclear-weapons program under way, no ifs or buts. For the next eighteen months or so, before it's running, we have the opportunity to blow it up. But this Iraq adventure will give blowing up your enemies a bad name. The concern now has to be that the 'Iraq syndrome' will make us flinch from blowing up people who really need to be blown up."

Bombing North Korea's reactor has never been an option, since North Korea has so many retaliatory forces so close to Seoul. But whatever choices the United States had at the beginning of 2002, it has fewer and worse ones now. The North Koreans are that much further along in their program; the U.S. military is under that much more strain; international hostility to U.S. policies is that much greater. "At the rate North Korea is pumping out bomb material," Pike said, "the Japanese will realize that the missile defense we've sold them will not save them. And they will conclude that only weaponizing their plutonium will enable them to sleep easily at night. And then you'll have South Korea and Taiwan . . ." and on through other ripple-effect scenarios. Pike says that the United States has little leverage to prevent any of this, and therefore can't afford to waste any more time in acting against North Korea.

"Are we better off in basic security than before we invaded Iraq?" asks Jeffrey Record, a professor of strategy at the Air War College and the author of the recent *Dark Victory*, a book about the Iraq War. "The answer is no. An unnecessary war has consumed American Army and other ground resources, to the point where we have nothing left in the cupboard for another contingency—for instance, should the North Koreans decide that with the Americans completely absorbed in Iraq, now is the time to do something."

"We really have four armies," an army officer involved in Pentagon planning for the Iraq War told me. "There's the one that's deployed in Afghanistan and Iraq. There's the one that's left back home in Fort Hood and other places. There's the 'modular army,' of new brigade-sized units that are supposed to be rotated in and out of locations easily. There's the Guard and Reserve. And every one of them is being chewed up by the ops tempo." "Ops tempo" means the pace of operations, and when it is too high, equipment and supplies are being used faster than they can be replaced, troops are being deployed far longer than they expected, and training is being pared back further than it should. "We're really in dire straits with resourcing," he said. "There's not enough armor for Humvees. There's not enough fifty-caliber machine guns for the 101st Airborne or the Tenth Mountain Division. A country that can't field heavy machine guns for its army—there's something wrong with the way we're doing business."

"The stress of war has hit all the services, but none harder than the army," Sydney Freedberg wrote recently in *National Journal*. "The crucial shortfall is not in money or machines, but in manpower." More than a third of the army's 500,000 active-duty soldiers are in Iraq or Kuwait. Freedberg referred to a study showing that fifteen of the army's thirty-four active-duty combat units were currently deployed overseas, and wrote, "That means that nearly as many units are abroad as at home, when historical experience shows that a long-term commitment, as with the British in Northern Ireland, requires three or four units recuperating and training for each one deployed." In the long run the U.S. military needs either more people or fewer responsibilities. At the moment, because of Iraq, it has very little slack for dealing with other emergencies that might arise.

WINTER: MISREADING THE ENEMY

President Bush's first major speech after 9/11, on September 20, 2001, was one of the outstanding addresses given by a modern president. But it introduced a destructive concept that Bush used more and more insistently through 2002. "Why do they hate us?" he asked about the terrorists. He answered that they hate what is best in us: "They hate what we see right here in this chamber—a democratically elected government . . . They hate our freedoms—our freedom of religion, our freedom of speech, our freedom to vote and assemble and disagree with each other." As he boiled down this thought in subsequent comments it became "They hate us for who we are" and "They hate us because we are free."

There may be people who have studied, fought against, or tried to infiltrate al-Qaeda and who agree with Bush's statement. But I have never met any. The soldiers, spies, academics, and diplomats I have interviewed are unanimous in saying that "They hate us for who we are" is dangerous claptrap. Dangerous because it is so lazily self-justifying and self-deluding: the only thing we could possibly be doing wrong is being so excellent. Claptrap because it reflects so little knowledge of how Islamic extremism has evolved.

"There are very few people in the world who are going to kill themselves so we can't vote in the Iowa caucuses," Michael Scheuer said to me. "But there's a lot of them who are willing to die because we're helping the Israelis, or because we're helping Putin against the Chechens, or because we keep oil prices low so Muslims lose money." Jeffrey Record said, "Clearly they do not like American society.

They think it's far too libertine, democratic, Christian. But that's not the reason they attack us. If it were, they would have attacked a lot of other Western countries too. I don't notice them putting bombs in Norway. It's a combination of who we are and also our behavior."

The 2004 report of the 9/11 Commission, without associating this view with Bush, was emphatic in rejecting the "hate us for who we are" view. The commission said this about the motivation of Khalid Sheikh Muhammad, whom it identified as the "mastermind of the 9/11 attacks": "KSM's animus toward the United States stemmed not from his experiences there as a student, but rather from his violent disagreement with U.S. foreign policy favoring Israel." In discussing long-term strategies for dealing with extremist groups the commission said, "America's policy choices have consequences. Right or wrong, it is simply a fact that American policy regarding the Israeli–Palestinian conflict and American actions in Iraq are dominant staples of popular commentary across the Arab and Muslim world." The most striking aspect of the commission's analysis is that it offered any thoughts at all about the right long-term response to Islamic extremists. The 9/11 Commission was one of several groups seeking to fill the void left by the administration's failure to put forward any comprehensive battle plan for a long-term campaign against terrorism. By its actions the administration showed that the only terrorism problem it recognized was Saddam Hussein's regime, plus the al-Qaeda leaders shown on its "most wanted" lists.

The distinction between who we are and what we do matters, because it bears on the largest question about the

Iraq War: Will it bring less or more Islamic terrorism? If violent extremism is purely vengeful and irrational, there is no hope except to crush it. Any brutality along the way is an unavoidable cost. But if it is based on logic of any sort, a clear understanding of its principles could help us to weaken its appeal—and to choose tactics that are not self-defeating.

A later article will describe insights about controlling terrorism.* For now the point is the strong working-level consensus that terrorists are "logical," if hideously brutal, and that the steps in 2002 that led to war have broadened the extremists' base. In March 2003, just after combat began in Iraq, President Hosni Mubarak of Egypt warned that if the United States invaded, "instead of having one bin Laden, we will have one hundred bin Ladens." Six months later, when the combat was over, Rumsfeld wrote in a confidential memo quoted in *Plan of Attack,* "We lack metrics to know if we are winning or losing the global war on terror. Are we capturing, killing, or deterring and dissuading more terrorists every day than the madrassas [Islamic schools] and the radical clerics are recruiting, training, and deploying against us? . . . The cost-benefit ratio is against us! Our cost is billions against the terrorists' costs of millions." Six months after that, as violence surged in occupied Iraq, the International Institute for Strategic Studies in London reported that al-Qaeda was galvanized by the wars in Afghanistan and

---

*The article, which is not included in this volume, was published in the January–February 2005 issue of the *Atlantic* as "Success Without Victory: A Strategy of Containment for the Age of Terror."

Iraq. As of mid-2004 it had at least 18,000 operatives in sixty countries. "Al Qaeda has fully reconstituted [and] set its sights firmly on the USA and its closest Western allies in Europe," the report said. Meanwhile, a British parliamentary report warns that Afghanistan is likely to "implode" for lack of support.

"I have been saying for years, Osama bin Laden could never have done it without us," a civilian adviser to the Pentagon told me in summer of 2004. "We have continued to play to his political advantage and to confirm, in the eyes of his constituency, the very claims he made about us." Those claims are that the United States will travel far to suppress Muslims, that it will occupy their holy sites, that it will oppose the rise of Islamic governments, and that it will take their resources. "We got to Baghdad," Michael Scheuer said, "and the first thing Rumsfeld said is, 'We'll accept any government as long as it's not Islamic.' It draws their attention to bin Laden's argument that the United States is leading the West to annihilate Islam." The administration had come a long way from the end-of-Ramadan ceremony at the White House.

WHAT HAPPENED IN A YEAR

To govern is to choose, and the choices made in 2002 were fateful. The United States began that year shocked and wounded, but with tremendous strategic advantages. Its population was more closely united behind its leadership than it had been in fifty years. World opinion was strongly sympathetic. Longtime allies were eager to help; longtime antagonists were silent. The federal budget was nearly in balance, making ambitious projects feasible. The U.S. military was superbly equipped, trained, and prepared. An immediate foe was evident—and vulnerable—in Afghanistan. For the longer-term effort against Islamic extremism the administration could draw on a mature school of thought from academics, regional specialists, and its own intelligence agencies. All that was required was to think broadly about the threats to the country, and creatively about the responses.

The Bush administration chose another path. Implicitly at the beginning of 2002, and as a matter of formal policy by the end, it placed all other considerations second to regime change in Iraq. It hampered the campaign in Afghanistan before fighting began and wound it down prematurely, along the way losing the chance to capture Osama bin Laden. It turned a blind eye to misdeeds in Saudi Arabia and Pakistan, and to WMD threats from North Korea and Iran far more serious than any posed by Saddam Hussein, all in the name of moving toward a showdown with Iraq. It overused and wore out its army in invading Iraq—without committing enough troops for a successful occupation. It saddled the United States with ongoing costs that dwarf its spending for domestic security. And by every available measure it only worsened the risk of future terrorism. In every sense 2002 was a lost year.

WHY IRAQ HAS NO ARMY

DECEMBER 2005

When Saddam Hussein fell, the Iraqi people gained freedom. What they didn't get was public order. Looting
began immediately, and by the time it abated, signs of an insurgency had appeared. Four months after the invasion the
first bomb that killed more than one person went off; two
years later, through the summer of 2005, multiple-fatality
bombings occurred on average once a day. The targets were
not just U.S. troops but Iraqi civilians and, more important,
Iraqis who would bring order to the country. The first major
attack on Iraq's own policemen occurred in October 2003,
when a car bomb killed ten people at a Baghdad police station. In mid-2005 an average of ten Iraqi policemen or soldiers were killed each day. It is true, as U.S. officials often
point out, that the violence is confined mainly to four of
Iraq's eighteen provinces. But these four provinces contain
the nation's capital and just under half its people.

The crucial need to improve security and order in Iraq
puts the United States in an impossible position. It can't
honorably leave Iraq—as opposed to simply evacuating

Saigon-style—so long as its military must provide most of the manpower, weaponry, intelligence systems, and strategies being used against the insurgency. But it can't sensibly stay when the very presence of its troops is a worsening irritant to the Iraqi public and a rallying point for nationalist opponents—to say nothing of the growing pressure in the United States for withdrawal.

Therefore one question now trumps others in America's Iraq policy: whether the United States can foster the development of viable Iraqi security forces, both military and police units, to preserve order in a new Iraqi state.

The Bush administration's policy toward Iraq is based on the premise that this job can be done—and done soon enough to relieve the pressures created by the large-scale U.S. presence in Iraq. These include strains on the U.S. military from its long overseas assignments, mounting political resistance in America because of the cost and casualties of the war, and resentment in Iraq about the open-ended presence of foreign occupation troops. This is why President Bush and other officials say so often, "As Iraqis stand up, we will stand down." American maximalists who want to transform Iraq into a democracy, American minimalists who want chiefly to get U.S. troops out as soon as possible, and everyone in between share an interest in the successful creation of Iraq's own military.

If the United States can foster the development of a sufficiently stable political system in Iraq, and if it can help train, equip, and support military and police forces to defend that system, then American policy has a chance of succeeding.

The United States can pull its own troops out of Iraq, knowing that it has left something sustainable behind. But if neither of those goals is realistic—if Iraqi politics remains chaotic and the Iraqi military remains overwhelmed by the insurgent threat—then the American strategy as a whole is doomed.

As Iraqi politicians struggle over terms of a new constitution, Americans need to understand the military half of the long-term U.S. strategy: when and whether Iraqi forces can "stand up."

Early in the occupation American officials acted as if the emergence of an Iraqi force would be a natural process. "In less than six months we have gone from zero Iraqis providing security to their country to close to a hundred thousand Iraqis," Donald Rumsfeld said in October 2003. "Indeed, the progress has been so swift that . . . it will not be long before [Iraqi security forces] will be the largest and outnumber the U.S. forces, and it shouldn't be too long thereafter that they will outnumber all coalition forces combined." By the end of 2005 the count of Iraqi security forces should indeed surpass the total of American, British, and other coalition troops in Iraq. Police officers, controlled by Iraq's Ministry of the Interior, should number some 145,000. An additional 85,000 members of Iraq's army, plus tiny contingents in its navy and air force, should be ready for duty, under the control of Iraq's Ministry of Defense. Since early this year Iraqi units have fought more and more frequently alongside U.S. troops.

But most assessments from outside the administration

have been far more downbeat than Rumsfeld's. Time and again since the training effort began, inspection teams from Congress, the Government Accountability Office (GAO), think tanks, and the military itself have visited Iraq and come to the same conclusion: the readiness of many Iraqi units is low, their loyalty and morale are questionable, regional and ethnic divisions are sharp, and their reported numbers overstate their real effectiveness.

The numbers are at best imperfect measures. Early in 2005 the American-led training command shifted its emphasis from simple head counts of Iraqi troops to an assessment of unit readiness based on a four-part classification scheme. Level 1, the highest, was for "fully capable" units—those that could plan, execute, and maintain counterinsurgency operations with no help whatsoever. In the summer of 2004 Pentagon officials said that three Iraqi units, out of a total of 115 police and army battalions, had reached this level. In September the U.S. military commander in Iraq, Army General George Casey, lowered that estimate to one.

Level 2 was for "capable" units, which can fight against insurgents as long as the United States provides operational assistance (air support, logistics, communications, and so on). Marine General Peter Pace, who is now the chairman of the Joint Chiefs of Staff, said in the summer of 2004 that just under one-third of Iraqi army units had reached this level. A few more had by fall. Level 3, for "partially capable" units, included those that could provide extra manpower in efforts planned, led, supplied, and sustained by Americans. The remaining two-thirds of Iraqi army units, and half the police, were in this category. Level 4, "incapable" units, were those that were of no help whatsoever in fighting the insurgency. Half of all police units were so classified.

In short, if American troops disappeared tomorrow, Iraq would have essentially no independent security force. Half its policemen would be considered worthless, and the other half would depend on external help for organization, direction, and support.* Two-thirds of the army would be in the same dependent position, and even the better-prepared one-third would suffer significant limitations without foreign help.

The moment when Iraqis can lift much of the burden from American troops is not yet in sight. Understanding whether this situation might improve requires understanding what the problems have been so far.

Over the summer and fall of 2005 I asked a large number of people why Iraq in effect still had no army, and what, realistically, the United States could expect in the future. Most were Americans, but I also spoke with experts from Iraq, Britain, Israel, France, and other countries. Most had served in the military; a large number had recently been posted in Iraq, and a sizable contingent had fought in Vietnam. Almost all those still on active duty insisted that I not use their

---

*By the spring of 2006, four months after this article appeared, the shortcomings of the Iraqi police force were growing more and more apparent. The new Iraqi army continued its gradual improvements. But the police, which are at least as important as regular army troops in any counterinsurgency effort, were often corrupt, controlled by ethnic militias, and infiltrated by insurgents. They were therefore of little use in controlling the violence in Baghdad and other cities.

names. The army's press office did arrange for me to speak with Lieutenant General Dave Petraeus, who was just completing his year's assignment as commander of the training effort in Iraq, before being replaced by Martin Dempsey, another three-star army general. But it declined requests for interviews with Petraeus's predecessor, Major General Paul Eaton, or others who had been involved in training programs during the first months of the occupation, or with lower-ranking officers and enlisted men. Many of them wanted to talk or correspond anyway.

What I heard amounted to this: The United States has recently figured out a better approach to training Iraqi troops. Early in 2005 it began putting more money, and more of its best people, on the job. As a result, more Iraqi units are operating effectively, and fewer are collapsing or deserting under pressure. In 2004, during major battles in Fallujah, Mosul, and elsewhere, large percentages of the Iraqi soldiers and policemen supposedly fighting alongside U.S. forces simply fled when the shooting began. But since the Iraqi elections last January "there has not been a single case of Iraqi security forces melting away or going out the back door of the police station," Petraeus told me. Iraqi recruits keep showing up at police and military enlistment stations, even as service in police and military units has become more dangerous.

But as the training and numbers are getting somewhat better, the problems created by the insurgency are getting worse—and getting worse faster than the Iraqi forces are improving. Measured against what it would take to leave Iraqis fully in charge of their own security, the United States and the Iraqi government are losing ground. Absent a dramatic change—in the insurgency, in American efforts, in resolving political differences in Iraq—America's options will grow worse, not better, as time goes on. Here is a sampling of worried voices:

"The current situation will NEVER allow for an effective ISF [Iraqi Security Force] to be created," a young Marine Corps officer who will not let me use his name wrote in an e-mail after he returned from Iraq this summer. "We simply do not have enough people to train forces. If we shift personnel from security duties to training, we release newly trained ISF into ever-worsening environs."

"A growing number of U.S. military officers in Iraq and those who have returned from the region are voicing concern that the nascent Iraqi army will fall apart if American forces are drawn down in the foreseeable future," Elaine Grossman, of the well-connected newsletter *Inside the Pentagon,* reported in September.

"U.S. trainers have made a heroic effort and have achieved some success with some units," Ahmed Hashim, of the Naval War College, told me in an e-mail. "But the Iraqi Security Forces are almost like a black hole. You put a lot in and little comes back out."

"I have to tell you that corruption is eating the guts of this counterinsurgency effort," a civilian wrote in an e-mail from Baghdad. Money meant to train new troops was leaking out to terrorists, he said. He empathized with "Iraqi officers here who see and yet are powerless to stop it because of the corrupt ministers and their aides."

"On the current course we will have two options," I was told by a lieutenant colonel who had recently served in Iraq and who prefers to remain anonymous. "We can lose in Iraq and destroy our army, or we can just lose."

The officer went on to say that of course neither option was acceptable, which is why he thought it so urgent to change course. By "destroy our army" he meant that it would take years for the U.S. military to recover from the strain on manpower, equipment, and—most of all—morale that staying in Iraq would put on it. (Retired Army General Barry McCaffrey had this danger in mind when he told *Time* magazine early in 2005 that "the army's wheels are going to come off in the next twenty-four months" if it remained in Iraq.) "Losing" in Iraq would mean failing to overcome the violent insurgency. A continuing insurgency would, in the view of the officer I spoke with, sooner or later mean the country's fracture in a bloody civil war. That, in turn, would mean the emergence of a central "Sunni-stan" more actively hostile to the United States than Saddam Hussein's Iraq ever was, which could in the next decade be what the Taliban of Afghanistan was in the 1990s: a haven for al-Qaeda and related terrorists. "In Vietnam we just lost," the officer said. "This would be losing with consequences."

How the Iraq story turns out will not be known for years,

but based on what is now knowable, the bleak prospect today is the culmination of a drama's first three acts. The first act involves neglect and delusion. Americans—and Iraqis—will spend years recovering from decisions made or avoided during the days before and after combat began, and through the first year of the occupation. The second act involves a tentative approach to a rapidly worsening challenge during the occupation's second year. We are now in the third act, in which Americans and Iraqis are correcting earlier mistakes but too slowly and too late.

As for the fourth act, it must resolve the tensions created in the previous three.

I. AUTUMN 2002–AUTUMN 2003: TAKEN BY SURPRISE

"It was clear what might happen in a highly militarized society once the regime fell," Anthony Cordesman wrote recently. Cordesman, of the Center for Strategic and International Studies, in Washington, has produced an authoritative series of reports on the new Iraqi military, available at the CSIS Web site. "The U.S. chose to largely ignore these indicators."

In explaining the early failures that plagued the occupation, Cordesman cited factors that have become familiar: an unrealistic expectation of how long Iraqis would welcome a foreign force; a deliberate decision to hold down the size of the invading army; too little preparation for postwar complications; and so on. Before the invasion Saddam Hussein had employed at least half a million soldiers and policemen to keep the lid on Iraq. The United States went in with less than a third that many troops, and because virtually none of them spoke Arabic, they could rarely detect changes in the Iraqi mood or exert influence except by force.

But the explanation of early training problems also leads in some less familiar directions. One view about why things went so wrong so fast is espoused by Ahmed Chalabi, one-time leader of the Iraqi National Congress, and American supporters of the war such as James Woolsey, a former CIA director, and Richard Perle, a former chairman of the Defense Policy Board. "My view is pretty straightforward," Woolsey told me. "We lost five years, thanks to the State Department and the CIA." The years in question were from 1998, when Congress passed and Bill Clinton signed the Iraq Liberation Act, advocating regime change in Iraq, to 2003, when U.S. troops moved on Baghdad. The act provided $97 million for arms and for training expatriate Iraqi forces. "All we had to do was use some of that money to train mainly Kurdish and Shia units to fight with us, like the Free French in 1944," Woolsey said. The main counterargument is that a Kurdish-Shiite invading army would have made it even harder to deal with Sunnis after Saddam fell.

A different view is strongly held by others among the war's early advocates within the Bush administration. In discussions with former members of the administration I was told they felt truly bad about only one intelligence failure. It did not concern WMD stockpiles in Iraq; the world's other intelligence agencies all made the same mistake, my informants said, and Saddam Hussein would have kept trying to build them anyway. What bothered them was that they did not grasp that he was planning all along to have his army melt away and reemerge as a guerrilla force once the Americans took over. In this view the war against Saddam's "bitter enders" is still going on, and the new Iraqi forces are developing as fast or as slowly as anyone could expect.

But here is the view generally accepted in the military: the war's planners, military and civilian, took the postwar transition too much for granted; then they made a grievous error in suddenly dismissing all members of the Iraqi army; and then they were too busy with other emergencies and routines to think seriously about the new Iraqi army.

"Should we have had training teams ready to go the day we crossed the border?" asks Lieutenant General Jim Mattis, who commanded the First Marine Division during the assault on Iraq (and whom Harrison Ford is scheduled to play in a film about the battle of Fallujah). "Of course! The military has one duty in a situation like this, and that is to provide security for the indigenous people. It's the windbreak behind which everything else can happen." Mattis argued before the war that teams of civic advisers should have been ready to flood in: mayors from North America and Europe to work with Iraqi mayors, police chiefs with police chiefs, all with the goal of preparing the locals to provide public order. "But we didn't do it, and the bottom line was the loss of security."

Many other people suggest many other sins of omission in preparations for the war. But at least one aspect of the transition was apparently given careful thought: how to handle the Iraqi military once it had surrendered or been defeated. Unfortunately, that careful thought was ignored or overruled.

After years of misuse under Saddam Hussein, the Iraqi military had severe problems, including bad morale, corrupt leadership, shoddy equipment, and a reputation for brutality. But the regular army numbered some 400,000 members, and if any of them could be put to use, there would be less work for Americans.

By late 2002, after Congress voted to authorize war if necessary, Jay Garner, a retired three-star army general, was thinking about how he might use some of these soldiers if the war took place and he became the first viceroy of Iraq. Garner, who had supervised Kurdish areas after the Gulf War, argued for incorporating much of the military rank-and-file into America's occupation force. Stripping off the top leadership would be more complicated than with, say, the Japanese or German army after World War II, because Iraq's army had more than 10,000 generals. (The U.S. Army, with about the same number of troops, has around 300 generals.) But, I was told by a former senior official who was closely involved in making the plans, "the idea was that on balance it was much better to keep them in place and try to put them to work, public works–style, on reconstruction, than not to." He continued, "The advantages of using them were: They had organization. They had equipment, especially organic transport [jeeps, trucks], which let them get themselves from place to place. They had a structure. But it was a narrow call, because of all the disadvantages." Garner intended to put this plan into action when he arrived in

Baghdad in April 2003. He told me recently that there were few signs of the previous army when he first arrived. "But we sent out feelers, and by the first week in May we were getting a lot of responses back. We had a couple of Iraqi officers come to me and say, 'We could bring this division back, that division.' We began to have dialogues and negotiations."

Then, on May 23, came a decision that is likely to be debated for years: Coalition Provisional Authority Order Number 2, to disband the Iraqi military and simply send its members home without pay.

"I always begin with the proposition that this argument is entirely irrelevant," Walter Slocombe, the man usually given credit or blame for initiating the decision, told me in the summer. During the Clinton administration Slocombe was undersecretary for policy at the Pentagon, the job later made famous by Douglas Feith. A month after the fall of Baghdad, Slocombe went to the Green Zone as a security adviser to Paul Bremer, who had just replaced Garner as the ranking American civilian.

On arrival Slocombe advocated that the Coalition Provisional Authority, or CPA, should face the reality that the previous Iraqi army had disappeared. "There was no intact Iraqi force to 'disband,'" Slocombe said. "There was no practical way to reconstitute an Iraqi force based on the old army any more rapidly than has happened. The facilities were just destroyed, and the conscripts were gone and not coming back." The Bush administration officials who had previously instructed Garner to reconstitute the military endorsed Slocombe's view: the negative aspects of consorting with a corrupt, brutal force were still there, and the positives seemed to be gone. "All the advantages they had ran away with the soldiers," the senior official involved in the plans said. "The organization, the discipline, the organic transport. The facts had changed."

The arguments about the decision are bitter, and they turn on two points: whether the Iraqi army had in fact irreversibly "disbanded itself," as Slocombe contends, and whether the American authorities could have found some way to avoid turning the hundreds of thousands of discharged soldiers into an armed and resentful opposition group. "I don't buy the argument that there was no army to cashier," says Barak Salmoni, of the Marine Corps Training and Education Command. "It may have not been showing up to work, but I can assure you that they would have if there had been dollars on the table. And even if the Iraqi army did disband, we didn't have to alienate them"—mainly by stopping their pay. Several weeks later the Americans announced that they would resume some army stipends, but by then the damage had been done.

Garner was taken by surprise by the decision, and has made it clear that he considers it a mistake. I asked him about the frequently voiced argument that there was no place to house the army because the barracks had been wrecked. "We could have put people in hangars," he said. "That is where our troops were."

The most damaging criticism of the way the decision was made comes from Paul Hughes, who was then an army colonel on Garner's staff. "Neither Jay Garner nor I had been asked about the wisdom of this decree," Hughes recalls. He was the only person from Garner's administration then talking with Iraqi military representatives about the terms of their reengagement. On the eve of the order to disband, he says, more than 100,000 Iraqi soldiers had submitted forms to receive a onetime twenty-dollar emergency payment, from funds seized from Saddam's personal accounts, which they would show up to collect.

"My effort was not intended to reactivate the Iraqi military," Hughes says. "Whenever the Iraqi officers asked if they could re-form their units, I was quite direct with them that if they did, they would be attacked and destroyed. What we wanted to do was arrange the process by which these hundred thousand soldiers would register with [the occupation authorities], tell us what they knew, draw their pay, and then report to selected sites. CPA Order Number 2 simply stopped any effort to move forward, as if the Iraqi military had ceased to exist. [Walt Slocombe's] statement about the twenty dollars still sticks in my brain: 'We don't pay armies we defeated.' My Iraqi friends tell me that this decision was what really spurred the nationalists to join the infant insurgency. We had advertised ourselves as liberators and turned on these people without so much as a second thought."

The argument will go on. But about what happened next there is little dispute. Having eliminated the main existing security force, and having arrived with fewer troops than past experience in the Balkans, Germany, and Japan would suggest for so large a territory, American officials essentially wasted the next six months. By the time they thought seriously about reconstituting Iraq's military and police forces, the insurgency was under way and the challenge of pacifying Iraq had magnified.

There is no single comprehensive explanation for what went wrong. After the tension leading up to the war and the brilliant, brief victory, political and even military leaders seemed to lose interest, or at least intensity. "Once Baghdad was taken, Tommy Franks checked out," Victor O'Reilly, who has written extensively about the U.S. military, told me. "He seemed to be thinking mainly about his book." Several people I spoke with volunteered this view of Franks, who was the CentCom commander during the war. (Franks did not respond to interview requests, including those sent through his commercially minded Web site, TommyFranks.com.) In retrospect the looting was the most significant act of the first six months after the war. It degraded daily life, especially in Baghdad, and it made the task of restoring order all the more difficult for the U.S. or Iraqi forces that would eventually undertake it. But at the time neither political nor military leaders treated it as urgent. Weeks went by before U.S. troops effectively intervened.

In June 2003, as the looting was dying down but the first signs of insurgent violence were appearing, the CSIS sent a team of experts who had worked in past occupations. They were alarmed by what they saw. "There is a general sense of steady deterioration in the security situation, in Baghdad, Mosul, and elsewhere," they reported. "Virtually every Iraqi and most CPA and coalition military officials as well as most contractors we spoke to cited the lack of public safety as their number one concern." At that time, the team pointed out, some five thousand U.S. troops were tied down guarding buildings in Baghdad, with two and a half battalions, representing well over a thousand troops, guarding the American headquarters alone.

Anthony Cordesman, of the CSIS, says there was never a conscious decision to delay or ignore training, but at any given moment in the occupation's first months some other goal always seemed more urgent or more interesting. Through the first six months of the occupation capturing Saddam Hussein seemed to be the most important step toward ending the resistance. His two sons were killed in July; he himself was captured in December; and the insurgency only grew. Along the way the manhunt relied on detention, interrogation, and break-down-doors-at-night techniques that hastened resentment of the U.S. presence. "The search for Saddam colored everything," Victor O'Reilly told me. "It is my belief that the insurgency was substantially created by the tactics used by the occupying force, who were initially the saviors, in their search for Saddam. Ambitious generals, who should have known better, created a very aggressive do-what-is-necessary culture. Frustrated troops, with no familiarity with the language or culture, naturally make mistakes. And in a tribal society if you shoot one person it spreads right through the system."

The hunt for WMD troves, conducted in the same way as the search for Saddam and by troops with the same inability to understand what was being said around them, had a similar embittering effect. The junior-level soldiers and marines

163

I interviewed consistently emphasized how debilitating the language barrier was. Having too few interpreters, they were left to communicate their instructions with gestures and sign language. The result was that American troops were blind and deaf to much of what was going on around them, and the Iraqis were often terrified.

General Mattis had stressed to his troops the importance of not frightening civilians, so as not to turn those civilians into enemies. He, too, emphasizes the distractions in the first year that diminished the attention paid to building an Iraqi security force. "There was always something," he told me. "Instead of focusing on security, we were trying to get oil pipelines patched, electrical grids back into position, figure out who the engineers were we could trust, since some of them hated us so much they would do sabotage work. It was going to take a while."

When Americans did think about a new Iraqi army, they often began with fears that it might become too strong too fast. "Everybody assumed that within Iraq it would be peaceful," says T. X. Hammes, the author of *The Sling and the Stone,* who was then in Iraq as a Marine Corps colonel. "So the biggest concern was reassuring all of Iraq's neighbors that Iraq would not be a threat. One of the ways you do that is by building a motor infantry force with no logistics"—that is, an army that can't sustain any large-scale offensive operation. Such an army might assuage concerns in Syria and Iran, but it would do little to provide internal security, and would not be prepared for domestic counterinsurgency work. (This tension has not been resolved: to this day the Iraqi government complains that the United States will not help it get adequate tanks, armored vehicles, and artillery.) Corrupt use of U.S. aid and domestic Iraqi resources was a constant and destructive factor. Last August the Knight Ridder newspapers revealed that Iraq's Board of Supreme Audit had surveyed arms contracts worth $1.3 billion and concluded that about $500 million had simply disappeared in payoffs, kickbacks, and fraud.

Training the police would be as big a challenge as training the army. "There was no image of a noncorrupt police force anywhere in the country," Mattis says. And to make matters more difficult, the effort began just as the police were coming under attack from insurgents' bombs and grenades.

Throughout the occupation, but most of all in these early months, training suffered from a "B-Team" problem. Before the fighting there was a huge glamour gap in the Pentagon between people working on so-called Phase III—the "kinetic" stage, the currently fashionable term for what used to be called "combat"—and those consigned to thinking about Phase IV, postwar reconstruction. The gap persisted after Baghdad fell. Nearly every military official I spoke with said that formal and informal incentives within the military made training Iraqi forces seem like second-tier work.

There were exceptions. The Green Berets and other elite units of the Special Forces have long prided themselves on being able to turn ragtag foreign armies into effective fighting units. But there weren't enough Special Forces units to go around, and the mainstream Army and Marine Corps were far less enthusiastic about training assignments. Especially at the start, training missions were filled mostly by people who couldn't get combat postings, and by members of the Reserves and the National Guard.

Walter Slocombe told me that there could have been a larger structural attempt to deal with the B-Team issue. "If we knew then what we know now," he said—that is, if people in charge had understood that public order would be the biggest postwar problem, and that Iraqis would soon resent the presence of foreigners trying to impose that order— "we would have done things differently. It would have made sense to have had an American military unit assigned this way from the beginning. They would be told, 'You guys aren't going to fight this war. You're not going to get Medals of Honor. But you will get due recognition. Your job is to run the occupation and train the Iraqis.' And we'd configure for that mission."

But of course that didn't happen. "I couldn't believe that we weren't ready for the occupation," Terence Daly, a retired army colonel who learned the tactics of counterinsurgency in Vietnam, told me. "I was horrified when I saw the looting and the American inaction afterward. If I were an Iraqi, it would have shown me these people are not serious."

II. AUTUMN 2003–AUTUMN 2004: OVERWHELMED

By late 2003 the United States had lost time and had changed identity, from liberator to occupier. But in its public pronouncements and its internal guidance the administration resisted admitting, even to itself, that it now faced a genuine insurgency—one that might grow in strength— rather than merely facing the dregs of the old regime, whose power would naturally wane as its leaders were caught and killed. On June 16 Army General John Abizaid, newly installed as CentCom commander, was the first senior American official to say that in fact the United States now faced a "classical guerrilla-type campaign." Two days later, in congressional testimony, Paul Wolfowitz, the deputy secretary of defense, seemed to accept the definition, saying, "There is a guerrilla war there, but . . . we can win it." On June 30 Rumsfeld corrected both of them, saying that the evidence from Iraq "doesn't make it anything like a guerrilla war or an organized resistance." Two days after that President Bush said at a White House ceremony that some people felt that circumstances in Iraq were "such that they can attack us there. My answer is, Bring them on." Meanwhile, the insurgency in Iraq grew worse and worse.

Improving the training of Iraqis suddenly moved up the list of concerns. Karl Eikenberry, an army general who had trained Afghan forces after the fall of the Taliban, was sent to Iraq to see what was wrong. Pentagon briefers referred more and more frequently to the effort to create a new Iraqi military. By early 2004 the administration had decided to spend more money on troop training, and to make it more explicitly part of the U.S. mission in Iraq. It was then that a grim reality hit: how hard this process would actually be.

"Training is not just learning how to fire a gun," I was told by a congressional staff member who has traveled frequently to Afghanistan since 9/11. "That's a part of it, but only a small part." Indeed, basic familiarity with guns is an area in which Iraqis outdo Americans. Walter Slocombe says that the CPA tried to enforce a gun-control law—only one AK-47 per household—in the face of a widespread Iraqi belief that many families needed two, one for the house and one for traveling.

Everyone I interviewed about military training stressed that it was only trivially about teaching specific skills. The real goal was to transform a civilian into a soldier. The process runs from the individual level, to the small groups that must trust one another with their lives, to the combined units that must work in coordination rather than confusedly firing at one another, to the concept of what makes an army or a police force different from a gang of thugs.

"The simple part is individual training," Jay Garner says. "The difficult part is collective training. Even if you do a good job of all that, the really difficult thing is all the complex processes it takes to run an army. You have to equip it. You have to equip all units at one time. You have to pay them on time. They need three meals a day and a place to sleep. Fuel. Ammunition. These sound simple, but they're incredibly difficult. And if you don't have them, that's what makes armies not work."

In countless ways the trainers on site faced an enormous challenge. The legacy of Saddam Hussein was a big problem. It had encouraged a military culture in which officers were privileged parasites, enlisted soldiers were cannon fodder, and noncommissioned officers (NCOs)—the sergeants who make the U.S. military function—were barely known. "We are trying to create a professional NCO corps," Army Major Bob Bateman told me. "Such a thing has never existed anywhere in the region. Not in regular units, not in police forces, not in the military."

The ethnic and tribal fissures in Iraq were another big problem. Half a dozen times in my interviews I heard variants on this Arab saying: "Me and my brother against my cousin; me and my cousin against my village; me and my village against a stranger." "The thing that holds a military unit together is trust," T. X. Hammes says. "That's a society not based on trust." A young Marine Corps officer wrote in an e-mail, "Due to the fact that Saddam murdered, tortured, raped, etc. at will, there is a limited pool of 18- to 35-year-old males for service that are physically or mentally qualified for service. Those that are fit for service, for the most part, have a DEEP hatred for those not of the same ethnic or religious affiliation."

The Iraqi culture of guns was, oddly, not an advantage but another problem. It had created gangs, not organized troops. "It's easy to be a gunman and hard to be a soldier," one expert told me. "If you're a gunman, it doesn't matter if your gun shoots straight. You can shoot it in the general direction of people, and they'll run." Many American trainers refer to an Iraqi habit of "Inshallah firing," also called "death blossom" marksmanship. "That is when they pick it up and start shooting," an officer now on duty in Baghdad told me by phone. "Death just blossoms around them."

The constant attacks from insurgents were a huge problem, and not just in the obvious ways. The U.S. military tries hard to separate training from combat. Combat is the acid test, but over time it can, strangely, erode proficiency. Under combat pressure troops cut corners and do whatever it takes to survive. That is why when units return from combat, the Pentagon officially classifies them as "unready" until they have rested and been retrained in standard procedures. In principle the training of Iraqi soldiers and policemen should take place away from the battlefield, but they are under attack from the moment they sign up. The pressure is increased because of public hostility to the foreign occupiers. "I know an Iraqi brigade commander who has to take off his uniform when he goes home, so nobody knows what he's done," Barak Salmoni told me. The Iraqi commander said to him, "It really tugs at our minds that we have to worry about our families' dying in the insurgency when we're fighting the insurgency somewhere else." The GAO found that in these circumstances security units from "troubled townships" often deserted en masse.

The United States, too, brought its own range of problems. One was legislative. Because U.S. forces had helped prop up foreign dictators, Congress in the 1970s prohibited most forms of American aid to police forces—as distinct from armies—in other countries. For the purposes of containing the insurgency in Iraq the distinction was meaningless. But administration officials used up time and energy through 2004 figuring out an answer to this technical-sounding yet important problem.

Language remained a profound and constant problem. One of the surprises in asking about training Iraqi troops was how often it led to comparisons with Vietnam. Probably because everything about the Vietnam War took longer to develop, "Vietnamization" was a more thought-through, developed strategy than "Iraqization" has had a chance to be. A notable difference is that Americans chosen for training assignments in Vietnam were often given four to six months of language instruction. That was too little to produce any real competence, but enough to provide useful rudiments that most Americans in Iraq don't have.

The career patterns of the U.S. military were a problem. For family reasons, and to keep moving up in rank, American soldiers rotate out of Iraq at the end of a year. They may be sent back to Iraq, but probably on a different assignment in a different part of the country. The adviser who has been building contacts in a village or with a police unit is gone, and a fresh, non-Arabic-speaking face shows up. "All the relationships an adviser has established, all the knowledge he has built up, goes right with him," Terence Daly, the counterinsurgency specialist from the Vietnam War, says. Every manual on counterinsurgency emphasizes the need for long-term personal relations. "We should put out a call for however many officers and NCOs we need," Daly says, "and give them six months of basic Arabic. In the course of this training we could find the ones suited to serve there for five years. Instead we treat them like widgets."

All indications from the home front were that training Iraqis had become a boring issue. Opponents of the war rarely talked about it. Supporters reeled off encouraging but hollow statistics as part of a checklist of successes the press failed to report. President Bush placed no emphasis on it in his speeches. Donald Rumsfeld, according to those around him, was bored by Iraq in general and this tedious process in particular, neither of which could match the challenge of transforming America's military establishment.*

The lack of urgency showed up in such mundane ways as equipment shortages. In the spring of 2004 investigators from the GAO found that the Iraqi police had only 41 percent of the patrol vehicles they needed, 21 percent of the handheld radios, and 9 percent of the protective vests. The Iraqi Civil Defense Corps, a branch of the military, had received no protective vests at all. According to the GAO report, "A multinational force assessment noted that Iraqis within the Iraqi Civil Defense Corps felt the multinational force never took them seriously, as exhibited by what they perceived as the broken promises and the lack of trust of the multinational force."

Although most people I spoke with said they had warm

---

*This article went to press for the *Atlantic* in early October 2005. Over the preceding year, the administration had done little to emphasize or re-explain its strategy in Iraq. Then, in mid-November 2005, Representative John Murtha made the first of several speeches calling for withdrawal from Iraq where, he said, the United States was trapped by "a flawed policy wrapped in illusion." Because Murtha was a decorated Marine Corps veteran and, although a Democrat, a longtime hawk in foreign policy, his criticism was highly publicized. By the end of November, the administration had released its "National Strategy for Victory in Iraq," and the president had begun a series of speeches laying out what he considered the signs of economic, political, and military progress in Iraq. That "National Strategy for Victory," which was essentially a collection of past statements about American goals, is available at http://www.whitehouse.gov/infocus/iraq/iraq_strategy_nov2005.html. The *Atlantic* article, with the title "Why Iraq Has No Army," appeared as the magazine's cover story in the first few days of November.

relations with many of their Iraqi counterparts, the lack of trust applied on the U.S. side as well. American trainers wondered how many of the skills they were imparting would eventually be used against them, by infiltrators or by soldiers who later changed sides. Iraq's Ministry of Defense has complained that the United States is supplying simpler equipment, such as AK-47s rather than the more powerful M4 rifles, and pickup trucks rather than tanks. Such materiel may, as U.S. officials stress, be far better suited to Iraq's current needs. It would also be less troublesome if Iraq and the United States came to be no longer on friendly terms.

And the biggest problem of all was the kind of war this new Iraqi army had to fight.

"Promoting disorder is a legitimate objective for the insurgent," a classic book about insurgency says: "It helps to disrupt the economy, hence to produce discontent; it serves to undermine the strength and the authority of the counterinsurgent [that is, government forces]. Moreover, disorder . . . is cheap to create and very costly to prevent. The insurgent blows up a bridge, so every bridge has to be guarded; he throws a grenade in a movie theater, so every person entering a public place has to be searched."

The military and political fronts are so closely connected, the book concludes, that progress on one is impossible without progress on the other: "Every military move has to be weighed with regard to its political effects, and vice versa."

This is not a book about Iraq. The book is *Counterinsurgency Warfare: Theory and Practice,* which was published nearly forty years ago by a French soldier and military analyst, David Galula, and is based on his country's experiences in Algeria and Vietnam.

Counterinsurgency scholarship has boomed among military intellectuals in the 2000s, as it did in the 1960s, and for the same reason: insurgents are the enemy we have to fight. "I've been reading a lot of T. E. Lawrence, especially through the tough times," Dave Petraeus said when I asked where he had looked for guidance during his year of supervising training efforts. An influential book on counterinsurgency by John Nagl, an army lieutenant colonel who commanded a tank unit in Iraq, is called *Learning to Eat Soup with a Knife*. That was Lawrence's metaphor for the skills needed to fight Arab insurgents.

"No modern army using conventional tactics has ever defeated an insurgency," Terence Daly told me. Conventional tactics boil down to killing the enemy. At this the U.S. military, with unmatchable firepower and precision, excels. "Classic counterinsurgency, however, is not primarily about killing insurgents; it is about controlling the population and creating a secure environment in which to gain popular support," Daly says.

From the vast and growing literature of counterinsurgency come two central points. One, of course, is the intertwining of political and military objectives: in the long run this makes local forces like the Iraqi army more potent than any foreigners; they know the language, they pick up subtle signals, they have a long-term stake. The other is that defeating an insurgency is the very hardest kind of warfare.

The United States cannot win this battle in Iraq. It hopes the Iraqis can.

Through the second year of occupation most of the indications were dark. An internal Pentagon report found, "The first Iraqi army infantry battalions finished basic training in early 2004 and were immediately required in combat without complete equipment" Absent-without-leave rates among regular army units were in double digits and remained so for the rest of the year.

I asked Robert Pape about the AWOL and desertion problems that had plagued Iraqi forces in Mosul, Fallujah, and elsewhere. Pape, of the University of Chicago, is the author of *Dying to Win,* a recent book about suicide terrorism. "Really, it was not surprising that this would happen," he said. "You were taking a force that had barely been stood up and asking it to do one of the most demanding missions possible: an offensive mission against a city. Even with a highly loyal force you were basically asking them to sacrifice themselves. Search and destroy would be one of the last things you would want them to do."

A GAO report showed the extent of the collapse. Fifty percent of the Iraqi Civil Defense Corps in the areas around Baghdad deserted in the first half of April. So did 30 percent of those in the northeastern area around Tikrit and the southeast near al-Kut. And so did 80 percent of the forces around Fallujah.

This was how things still stood on the eve of America's presidential election and the beginning of a new approach in Baghdad.

III. AUTUMN 2004–AUTUMN 2005:
PROGRESS BUT NO URGENCY

At the end of June 2004 Ambassador Bremer went home. His Coalition Provisional Authority ceased to exist, and an interim Iraqi government, under a prime minister selected by the Americans, began planning for the first nationwide elections, which were held in January 2005. The first U.S. ambassador to postwar Iraq, John D. Negroponte, was sworn in as Bremer left. And a new American Army general arrived to supervise the training of Iraqis: Dave Petraeus, who had just received his third star.

The appointment was noticed throughout the military. Petraeus, who holds a Ph.D. from Princeton, had led the 101st Airborne during its drive on Mosul in 2003 and is one of the military's golden boys. What I heard about him from other soldiers reminded me of what reporters used to hear about Richard Holbrooke from other diplomats: many people marveled at his ambition; few doubted his skills. Petraeus's new assignment suggested that training Iraqis had become a sexier and more important job. By all accounts Petraeus and Negroponte did a lot to make up for lost time in the training program.

Under Petraeus the training command abandoned an often ridiculed way of measuring progress. At first Americans had counted all Iraqis who were simply "on duty"—a total that swelled to more than 200,000 by March 2004. Petraeus introduced an assessment of "unit readiness," as noted earlier. Training had been underfunded in mid-2004, but more money and equipment started to arrive.

The training strategy also changed. More emphasis was put on embedding U.S. advisers with Iraqi units. Teams of Iraqi foot soldiers were matched with U.S. units that could provide the air cover and other advanced services they needed. To save money and reduce the chance of a coup, Saddam Hussein's soldiers had only rarely, or never, fired live ammunition during training. According to an unpublished study from the U.S. Army War College, even the elite units of the Baghdad Republican Guard were allowed to fire only about ten rounds of ammunition per soldier in the year before the war, versus about 2,500 rounds for the typical U.S. infantry soldier. To the amazement of Iraqi army veterans, Petraeus introduced live-fire exercises for new Iraqi recruits.

At the end of 2004, as the Iraqi national elections drew near, Negroponte used his discretion to shift $2 billion from other reconstruction projects to the training effort. "That will be seen as quite a courageous move, and one that paid big dividends," Petraeus told me. "It enabled the purchase of a lot of additional equipment, extra training, and more rebuilding of infrastructure, which helped us get more Iraqi forces out in the field by the January 30 elections."

The successful staging of the elections marked a turning point—at least for the training effort. Political optimism faded with the subsequent deadlocks over the constitution, but "we never lost momentum on the security front," Petraeus told me. During the elections more than 130,000 Iraqi troops guarded more than 5,700 polling stations; there were some attacks, but the elections went forward. "We have transitioned six or seven bases to Iraqi control," he continued, listing a variety of other duties Iraqi forces had assumed. "The enemy recognizes that if Iraqi security forces ever really get traction, they are in trouble. So all of this is done in the most challenging environment imaginable."

Had the training units avoided the "B-Team" taint? By e-mail I asked an officer on the training staff about the "loser" image traditionally attached to such jobs within the military. He wrote back that although training slots had long been seen as "career killers," the importance of the effort in Iraq was changing all that. From others not involved in training I heard a more guarded view: If an Iraqi army emerges, the image of training will improve; if it doesn't, the careers of Petraeus and his successor Dempsey will suffer.

Time is the problem. As prospects have brightened inside the training program, they have darkened across the country. From generals to privates, every soldier I spoke with stressed that the military campaign would ultimately fail without political progress. If an army has no stable government to defend, even the best-trained troops will devolve into regional militias and warlord gangs. "I always call myself a qualified optimist, but the qualification is Iraqi leaders muddling through," one senior officer told me. "Certain activities are beyond Americans' control."

Ethnic tensions divide Iraq, and they divide the new army. "Thinking that we could go in and produce a unified Iraqi army is like thinking you could go into the South after the Civil War and create an army of blacks and whites fighting side by side," Robert Pape, of the University of Chicago, told me. "You can pay people to go through basic training and take moderate risks. But unless they're really loyal to a government, as the risks go up, they will run." Almost every study of the new Iraqi military raises doubts about how loyally "Iraqi" it is, as opposed to Kurdish, Shiite, or Sunni. The most impressive successes by "Iraqi" forces have in fact been by units that were really Kurdish *peshmurga* or Shiite militias.

"There is still no sense of urgency," T. X. Hammes says. In August, he pointed out, the administration announced with pride that it had bought two hundred new armored vehicles for use in Iraq. "Two-plus years into the war, and we're proud! Can you imagine if in March of 1944 we had proudly announced two hundred new vehicles?" By 1944 American factories had been retooled to produce 100,000 warplanes. "From the president on down there is no urgency at all."

Since last June, President Bush has often repeated his "As Iraqi forces stand up . . ." formula, but he rarely says anything more specific about American exit plans.* When he welcomed Iraq's president, Jalal Talabani, to the White House in September, his total comment on the training issue in a substantial welcoming speech was "Our objective is to defeat the enemies of a free Iraq, and we're working to prepare more Iraqi forces to join the fight." This was followed

---

*As mentioned in the note on page 172, starting in November 2005 the president and other members of the administration spoke more often and in more detail about long-term plans for Iraq. At a press conference in March 2006, President Bush said that the ultimate withdrawal of U.S. troops from Iraq would be up to "future [U.S.] presidents and future governments of Iraq," implying that troops would remain there at least through the end of his term.

by the stand up/stand down slogan. Vice President Cheney sounds similarly dutiful. ("Our mission in Iraq is clear," he says in his typical speech. "On the military side we are hunting down the terrorists and training Iraqi security forces so they can take over responsibility for defending their own country." He usually follows with the slogan but with no further details or thoughts.)

Donald Rumsfeld has the same distant tone. Condoleezza Rice and Paul Wolfowitz have moved on to different things. At various times since 9/11 members of the administration have acted as if catching Osama bin Laden, or changing Social Security, or saving Terri Schiavo, or coping with Hurricane Katrina, mattered more than any possible other cause. Creating an Iraqi military actually matters more than almost anything else. But the people who were intent on the war have lost interest in the only way out.

A young officer said, "You tell me who in the White House devotes full time to winning this war." The answer seems to be Meghan O'Sullivan, a former Brookings scholar who is now the president's special assistant for Iraq. As best I can tell from Nexis, other online news sources, and the White House Web site, since taking the job late last year, she has made no public speeches or statements about the war.

IV. HOW TO LEAVE WITH HONOR

Listening to the Americans who have tried their best to create an Iraqi military can be heartening. They send e-mails or call late at night Iraq time to report successes. A Web magazine published by the training command, called *The Advisor,* carries photos of American mentors working side by side with their Iraqi students, and articles about new training techniques. The Americans can sound inspired when they talk about an Iraqi soldier or policeman who has shown bravery and devotion in the truest way—by running toward battle rather than away from it, or rushing to surround a suicide bomber and reduce the number of civilians who will be killed.

But listening to these soldiers and advisers is also deeply discouraging—in part because so much of what they report is discouraging in itself, but even more because the conversations head to a predictable dead end. Sooner or later the question is, What do we do now? or What is the way out? And the answer is that there is no good answer.

Let me suggest a standard for judging endgame strategies in Iraq, given the commitment the United States has already made. It begins with the recognition that even if it were possible to rebuild and fully democratize Iraq, as a matter of political reality the United States will not stay to see it through. (In Japan, Germany, and South Korea we did see it through. But while there were postwar difficulties in all those countries, none had an insurgency aimed at Americans.) But perhaps we could stay long enough to meet a more modest standard.

What is needed for an honorable departure is, at a minimum, a country that will not go to war with itself, and citizens who will not turn to large-scale murder. This requires

Iraqi security forces that are working on a couple of levels: a national army strong enough to deter militias from any region and loyal enough to the new Iraq to resist becoming the tool of any faction; policemen who are sufficiently competent, brave, and honest to keep civilians safe. If the United States leaves Iraq knowing that non-American forces are sufficient to keep order, it can leave with a clear conscience—no matter what might happen a year or two later.

In the end the United States may not be able to leave honorably. The pressure to get out could become too great. But if we were serious about reconstituting an Iraqi military as quickly as possible, what would we do? Based on these interviews, I have come to this sobering conclusion: the United States can best train Iraqis, and therefore best help itself leave Iraq, only by making certain very long-term commitments to stay.

Some of the changes that soldiers and analysts recommend involve greater urgency of effort, reflecting the greater importance of making the training succeed. Despite brave words from the Americans on the training detail, the larger military culture has not changed to validate what they do. "I would make advising an Iraqi battalion more career-enhancing than commanding an American battalion," one retired marine officer told me. "If we were serious, we'd be gutting every military headquarters in the world, instead of just telling units coming into the country they have to give up 20 percent of their officers as trainers."

The U.S. military does everything in Iraq worse and slower than it could if it solved its language problems. It is unbelievable that American fighting ranks have so little help. Soon after Pearl Harbor the U.S. military launched major Japanese–language training institutes at universities and was screening draftees to find the most promising students. America has made no comparable effort to teach Arabic. Nearly three years after the invasion of Iraq the typical company of 150 or so U.S. soldiers gets by with one or two Arabic speakers. T. X. Hammes says that U.S. forces and trainers in Iraq should have about 22,000 interpreters, but they have nowhere near that many. Some 600,000 Americans can speak Arabic. Hammes has proposed offering huge cash bonuses to attract the needed numbers to Iraq.

In many other ways the flow of dollars and effort shows that the military does not yet take Iraq—let alone the training effort there—seriously. The Pentagon's main weapons-building programs are the same now that they were five years ago, before the United States had suffered one attack and begun two wars. From the Pentagon's policy statements, and even more from its budgetary choices, one would never guess that insurgency was our military's main challenge, and that its main strategic hope lay in the inglorious work of training foreign troops. Planners at the White House and the Pentagon barely imagined before the war that large numbers of U.S. troops would be in Iraq three years later. So most initiatives for Iraq have been stopgap—not part of a systematic effort to build the right equipment, the right skills, the right strategies, for a long-term campaign.

Some other recommended changes involve more explicit long-range commitments. When officers talk about the risk of "using up" or "burning out" the military, they mean that too many arduous postings, renewed too frequently, will drive career soldiers out of the military. The recruitment problems of the National Guard are well known. Less familiar to the public but of great concern in the military is the "third tour" phenomenon: A young officer will go for his first yearlong tour in Iraq or Afghanistan, and then his second. Facing the prospect of his third, he may bail out while he still has time to start another, less stressful career.

For the military's sake soldiers need to go to Iraq less often, and for shorter periods. But success in training Iraqis will require some Americans to stay there much longer. Every book or article about counterinsurgency stresses that it is an intimate, subjective, human business. Establishing trust across different cultures takes time. After 9/11 everyone huffed about the shocking loss of "human intelligence" at America's spy agencies. But modern American culture—technological, fluid, transient—discourages the creation of the slow-growing, subtle bonds necessary for both good spy work and good military liaison. The British had their India and East Asia hands, who were effective because they spent years in the field cultivating contacts. The American military has done something similar with its Green Berets. For the training effort to have a chance, many, many more regular soldiers will need to commit to long service in Iraq.

The United States will have to agree to stay in Iraq in another significant way. When U.S. policy changed from counting every Iraqi in uniform to judging how many whole units were ready to function, a triage decision was made. The Iraqis would not be trained anytime soon for the whole range of military functions; they would start with the most basic combat and security duties. The idea, as a former high-ranking administration official put it, was "We're building a spearhead, not the whole spear."

The rest of the spear consists of the specialized, often technically advanced functions that multiply the combat units' strength. These are as simple as logistics—getting food, fuel, ammunition, spare parts, where they are needed—and as complex as battlefield surgical units, satellite-based spy services, and air support from helicopters and fighter planes.

The United States is not helping Iraq develop many of these other functions. Sharp as the Iraqi spearhead may become, on its own it will be relatively weak. The Iraqis know their own territory and culture, and they will be fighting an insurgency, not a heavily equipped land army. But if they can't count on the Americans to keep providing air support, intelligence and communications networks, and other advanced systems, they will never emerge as an effective force. So the United States will have to continue to provide all this. The situation is ironic. Before the war insiders argued that sooner or later it would be necessary to attack, because the U.S. Air Force was being "strained" by its daily sorties over Iraq's no-fly zones. Now that the war is over, the United States has taken on a much greater open-ended obligation.

In sum, if the United States is serious about getting out of Iraq, it will need to reconsider its defense spending and operations rather than leaving them to a combination of inertia, Rumsfeld-led plans for "transformation," and emergency stopgaps. It will need to spend money for interpreters. It will need to create large new training facilities for American troops, as happened within a few months of Pearl Harbor, and enroll talented people as trainees. It will need to make majors and colonels sit through language classes. It will need to broaden the Special Forces ethic to much more of the military, and make clear that longer tours will be the norm in Iraq. It will need to commit air, logistics, medical, and intelligence services to Iraq—and understand that this is a commitment for years, not a temporary measure. It will need to decide that there are weapons systems it does not require and commitments it cannot afford if it is to support the ones that are crucial. And it will need to make these decisions in a matter of months, not years—before it is too late.

America's hopes today for an orderly exit from Iraq depend completely on the emergence of a viable Iraqi security force. There is no indication that such a force is about to emerge. As a matter of unavoidable logic, the United States must therefore choose one of two difficult alternatives: It can make the serious changes—including certain commitments to remain in Iraq for many years—that would be necessary to bring an Iraqi army to maturity. Or it can face the stark fact that it has no orderly way out of Iraq, and prepare accordingly.

WILL IRAN BE NEXT?

DECEMBER 2004

Throughout the summer and fall of 2004, barely mentioned in America's presidential campaign, Iran moved steadily closer to a showdown with the United States (and other countries) over its nuclear plans.

In June the International Atomic Energy Agency (IAEA) said that Iran had not been forthcoming about the extent of its nuclear programs. In July, Iran indicated that it would not ratify a protocol of the Nuclear Non-Proliferation Treaty giving inspectors greater liberty within its borders. In August the Iranian defense minister warned that if Iran suspected a foreign power—specifically the United States or Israel—of preparing to strike its emerging nuclear facilities, it might launch a preemptive strike of its own, of which one target could be the U.S. forces next door in Iraq. In September, Iran announced that it was preparing thirty-seven tons of uranium for enrichment, supposedly for power plants, and it took an even tougher line against the IAEA. In October it announced that it had missiles capable of hitting targets 1,250 miles away—as far as southeastern Europe to the west and India to the east. Also, an Iranian Foreign Ministry spokesman rejected a proposal by Senator John Kerry that if the United States promised to supply all the nuclear fuel Iran needed for peaceful power-generating purposes, Iran would stop developing enrichment facilities (which could also help it build weapons).* Meanwhile, the government of Israel kept sending subtle and not-so-subtle warnings that if Iran went too far with its plans, Israel would act first to protect itself, as it had in 1981 by bombing the Iraqi nuclear facility at Osirak.

Preoccupied as they were with Iraq (and with refighting Vietnam), the presidential candidates did not spend much time on Iran. But after the election the winner will have no choice. The decisions that a president will have to make about Iran are like those that involve Iraq—but harder. A regime at odds with the United States, and suspected of encouraging Islamic terrorists, is believed to be developing very destructive weapons. In Iran's case, however, the governmental hostility to the United States is longer-standing (the United States implicitly backed Saddam Hussein during the Iran–Iraq War of the 1980s), the ties to terrorist groups are clearer, and the evidence of an ongoing nuclear-weapons program is stronger. Iran is bigger, more powerful, and

---

*Late in 2005, the Russian government offered a variant of this plan to Iran. Iran could build nuclear plants to generate energy, as long as it left the reprocessing of nuclear fuel, and therefore the potential to develop nuclear weapons, in Russian hands on Russian soil. The Iranian government initially indicated some openness to the proposal, but in early 2006 it backed away.

richer than Iraq, and it enjoys more international legitimacy than Iraq ever did under Saddam Hussein. The motives and goals of Iran's mullah government have been even harder for U.S. intelligence agencies to understand and predict than Saddam Hussein's were. And Iran is deeply involved in America's ongoing predicament in Iraq. Shiites in Iran maintain close cultural and financial contacts with Iraqi Shiite communities on the other side of the nearly 1,000-mile border between the countries. So far Iraq's Shiites have generally been less resistant to the U.S. occupation than its Sunnis. Most American experts believe that if it wanted to, Iran could incite Iraqi Shiites to join the insurgency in far greater numbers.

As a preview of the problems Iran will pose for the next American president, and of the ways in which that president might respond, the *Atlantic* conducted a war game in the fall of 2004, simulating preparations for a U.S. assault on Iran.

"War game" is a catchall term used by the military to cover a wide range of exercises. Some games run for weeks and involve real troops maneuvering across oceans or terrain against others playing the role of the enemy force. Some are computerized simulations of aerial, maritime, or land warfare. Others are purely talking-and-thinking processes, in which a group of people in a room try to work out the best solution to a hypothetical crisis. Sometimes participants are told to stay "in role"—to say and do only what a secretary of state or an army brigade commander or an enemy strategist would most likely say and do in a given situation.

Other times they are told to express their own personal views. What the exercises have in common is the attempt to simulate many aspects of conflict—operational, strategic, diplomatic, emotional, and psychological—without the cost, carnage, and irreversibility of real war. The point of a war game is to learn from simulated mistakes in order to avoid making them if conflict actually occurs.

Our exercise was stripped down to the essentials. It took place in one room, it ran for three hours, and it dealt strictly with how an American president might respond, militarily or otherwise, to Iran's rapid progress toward developing nuclear weapons. It wasn't meant to explore every twist or repercussion of past U.S. actions and future U.S. approaches to Iran. Reports of that nature are proliferating more rapidly than weapons.

Rather, we were looking for what Sam Gardiner, a retired air force colonel, has called the "clarifying effect" of intense immersion in simulated decision-making. Such simulations are Gardiner's specialty. For more than two decades he has conducted war games at the National War College and many other military institutions. Starting in 1989, two years before the Gulf War and fourteen years before Operation Iraqi Freedom, he created and ran at least fifty exercises involving an attack on Iraq. The light-force strategy that General Tommy Franks used to take Baghdad in 2003 first surfaced in a war game Gardiner designed in the 1980s. In 2002, as the real invasion of Iraq drew near, Gardiner worked as a private citizen to develop nonclassified simulations of the situation that would follow the fall of Baghdad.

These had little effect on U.S. policy, but proved to be prescient about the main challenges in restoring order to Iraq.*

Gardiner told me that the war games he has run as a military instructor frequently accomplish as much as several standard lectures or panel discussions do in helping participants think through the implications of their decisions and beliefs. For our purposes he designed an exercise to force attention on the three or four main issues the next president will have to face about Iran, without purporting to answer all the questions the exercise raised.

The scenario he set was an imagined meeting of the "Principals Committee"—that is, the most senior national-security officials of the next administration. The meeting would occur as soon as either administration was ready to deal with Iran, but after a November meeting of the IAEA. In the real world the IAEA was in fact meeting in November, and had set a deadline for Iran to satisfy its demands by the time of the meeting. For the purposes of the simulation Iran is assumed to have defied the deadline. That is a safe bet in the real world as well.

And so our group of principals gathered, to provide their best judgment to the president. Each of them had direct experience in making similar decisions. In the role of CIA director was David Kay, who after the Gulf War went to Iraq as the chief nuclear-weapons inspector for the IAEA and the United Nations Special Commission (UNSCOM), and went

---

*This was the same "net assessment" prepared by Gardiner and discussed on pages 91–94 of this book.

back in June 2003 to lead the search for weapons of mass destruction. Kay resigned that post in January 2004, after concluding that there had been no weapons stockpiles at the time of the war.

Playing secretary of state were Kenneth Pollack, of the Brookings Institution, and Reuel Marc Gerecht, of the American Enterprise Institute. Although neither is active in partisan politics (nor is anyone else who served on the panel), the views they expressed about Iran in our discussion were fairly distinct, with Gerecht playing a more Republican role in the discussions, and Pollack a more Democratic one. (This was the war game's one attempt to allow for different outcomes in the election.)

Both Pollack and Gerecht are veterans of the CIA. Pollack was a CIA Iran-Iraq analyst for seven years, and later served as the National Security Council's director for Persian Gulf affairs during the last two years of the Clinton administration. In 2002 his book *The Threatening Storm: The Case for Invading Iraq* was highly influential in warning about the long-term weapons threat posed by Saddam Hussein. In January 2004, in *The Atlantic Monthly*, Pollack examined how prewar intelligence had gone wrong.) His book about U.S.–Iranian tensions, *The Persian Puzzle*, has just been published. Gerecht worked for nine years in the CIA's Directorate of Operations, where he recruited agents in the Middle East. In 1997, under the pseudonym Edward Shirley, he published *Know Thine Enemy: A Spy's Journey into Revolutionary Iran*, which described a clandestine trip. He has written frequently about Iran, Afghanistan, and the craft of intelligence for the *Atlantic* and other publications.

The simulated White House chief of staff was Kenneth Bacon, the chief Pentagon spokesman during much of the Clinton administration, who is now the head of Refugees International. Before the invasion Bacon was closely involved in preparing for postwar humanitarian needs in Iraq.

Finally, the secretary of defense was Michael Mazarr, a professor of national-security strategy at the National War College, who has written about preventing nuclear proliferation in Iran, among other countries, and has collaborated with Gardiner on previous war games.

This war game was loose about requiring players to stay "in role." Sometimes the participants expressed their institutions' views; other times they stepped out of role and spoke for themselves. Gardiner usually sat at the conference table with the five others and served as national security adviser, pushing his panel to resolve their disagreements and decide on recommendations for the president. Occasionally he stepped into other roles at a briefing podium. For instance, as the general in charge of Central Command (CentCom)—the equivalent of Tommy Franks before the Iraq War and John Abizaid now—he explained detailed military plans.

Over the years Gardiner has concluded that role-playing exercises usually work best if the participants feel they are onstage, being observed; this makes them take everything more seriously and try harder to perform. So the exercise was videotaped, and several people were invited to watch and comment on it. One was Graham Allison, of Harvard University's Kennedy School of Government, a leading scholar of presidential decision-making, who served as a

Pentagon official in the first Clinton administration, specializing in nuclear-arms control. His *Essence of Decision,* a study of how the Kennedy administration handled the 1962 Cuban Missile Crisis, is the classic work in its field; his latest book, which includes a discussion of Iran, is *Nuclear Terrorism: The Ultimate Preventable Catastrophe.* Two other observers were active-duty officers: Marine Corps Colonel Thomas X. Hammes, who has specialized in counterinsurgency and whose book about dealing with Iran (and many other challenges), *The Sling and the Stone,* was published in 2004; and Army Major Donald Vandergriff, whose most recent book, about reforming the internal culture of the army, is *The Path to Victory* (2002). The fourth observer was Herbert Striner, formerly of the Brookings Institution, who as a young analyst at an army think tank, Operations Research Organization, led a team devising limited-war plans for Iran—back in the 1950s. Striner's team developed scenarios for one other regional war as well: in French Indochina, later known as Vietnam.

Promptly at nine o'clock one Friday morning in September, Gardiner called his group of advisers to order. In his role as national security adviser he said that over the next three hours they needed to agree on options and recommendations to send to the president in the face of Iran's latest refusal to meet demands and the latest evidence of its progress toward nuclear weaponry. Gardiner had already decided what questions not to ask. One was whether the United States could tolerate Iran's emergence as a nuclear power. That is, should Iran be likened to Saddam Hussein's Iraq, in whose possession nuclear weapons would pose an unacceptable threat, or to Pakistan, India, or even North Korea, whose nuclear ambitions the United States regrets but has decided to live with for now? If that discussion were to begin, it would leave time for nothing else.

Gardiner also chose to avoid posing directly the main question the game was supposed to illuminate: whether and when the United States should seriously consider military action against Iran. If he started with that question, Gardiner said, any experienced group of officials would tell him to first be sure he had exhausted the diplomatic options. So in order to force discussion about what, exactly, a military "solution" would mean, Gardiner structured the game to determine how the panel assessed evidence of the threat from Iran; whether it was willing to recommend steps that would keep the option of military action open, and what that action might look like; and how it would make the case for a potential military strike to an audience in the United States and around the world.

Before the game began, Gardiner emphasized one other point about his approach, the importance of which would become clear when the discussions were over. He had taken pains to make the material he would present as accurate, realistic, and true to standard national-security practice as possible. None of it was classified, but all of it reflected the most plausible current nonclassified information he could obtain. The detailed plans for an assault on Iran had also been carefully devised. They reflected the present state of Pentagon thinking about the importance of technology, information networks, and Special Forces operations. Afterward participants who had sat through real briefings of this sort said that Gardiner's version was authentic.

His commitment to realism extended to presenting all his information in a series of PowerPoint slides, on which U.S. military planners are so dependent that it is hard to imagine how Dwight Eisenhower pulled off D-Day without them. PowerPoint's imperfections as a deliberative tool are well known. Its formulaic outline structure can overemphasize some ideas or options and conceal others, and the amateurish graphic presentation of data often impedes understanding. But any simulation of a modern military exercise would be unconvincing without it. Gardiner's presentation used PowerPoint for its explanatory function and as a spine for discussion, its best use.

In his first trip to the podium Gardiner introduced himself as the director of central intelligence (DCI). (That was David Kay's role too, but during this phase he just sat and listened.) His assignment was to explain what U.S. intelligence knew and didn't know about Iran's progress toward nuclear weapons, and what it thought about possible impediments to that progress—notably Israel's potential to launch a preemptive attack on Iran's nuclear sites.

"As DCI, I've got to talk about uncertainty," Gardiner began—the way future intelligence officers presumably will after the Iraq-WMD experience, when George Tenet, as CIA director, claimed that the case for Iraq's having weapons was a "slam dunk." "It's an important part of this problem. The [intelligence] community believes that Iran could have a nuclear weapon in three years." He let that sink in and then added ominously, "Unless they have something we don't know about, or unless someone has given them or sold them something we don't know about"—or unless, on top of these "known unknowns," some "unknown unknowns" were speeding the pace of Iran's program.

One response to imperfect data about an adversary is to assume the worst and prepare for it, so that any other outcome is a happy surprise. That was the recommendation of Reuel Gerecht, playing the conservative secretary of state. "We should assume Iran will move as fast as possible," he said several times. "It would be negligent of any American strategic planners to assume a slower pace." But that was not necessarily what the DCI was driving at in underscoring the limits of outside knowledge about Iran. Mainly he meant to emphasize a complication the United States would face in making its decisions. Given Iran's clear intent to build a bomb, and given the progress it has already made, sometime in the next two or three years it will cross a series of "red lines," after which the program will be much harder for outsiders to stop.

Iran will cross one of the red lines when it produces enough enriched uranium for a bomb, and another when it has weapons in enough places that it would be impossible to remove them in one strike. "Here's the intelligence dilemma," Gardiner said. "We are facing a future in which this is probably Iran's primary national priority. And we have these red lines in front of us, and we"—meaning the intelligence agencies—"won't be able to tell you when they cross them." Hazy knowledge about Iran's nuclear progress doesn't dictate assuming the worst, Gardiner said. But it does mean that time is not on America's side. At some point, relatively soon, Iran will have an arsenal that no outsiders can destroy, and America will not know in advance when that point has arrived.

Then the threat assessment moved to two wild-card factors: Iran's current involvement in Iraq, and Israel's potential involvement with Iran. Both complicate and constrain the options open to the United States, Gardiner said. Iran's influence on the Shiite areas of Iraq is broad, deep, and obviously based on a vastly greater knowledge of the people and customs than the United States can bring to bear. So far Iran has seemed to share America's interest in calming the Shiite areas, rather than have them erupt on its border. But if it needs a way to make trouble for the United States, one is at hand.

As for Israel, no one can be sure what it will do if threatened. Yet from the U.S. perspective, it looks as if a successful preemptive raid might be impossible—or at least so risky as to give the most determined Israeli planners pause. Partly this is because of the same lack of knowledge that handicaps the United States. When Menachem Begin dispatched Israeli fighter planes to destroy Iraq's Osirak plant, he knew there was only one target, and that if it was eliminated, Iraq's nuclear program would be set back for many years. In our scenario as in real life, the Americans thought Ariel Sharon and his successors could not be sure how many important targets were in Iran, or exactly where all of them were, or whether Israel could destroy enough of them to make the raid worth the international outrage and the likely counterattack. Plus, operationally it would be hard.

But for the purposes of our scenario, Israel kept up its threats to take unilateral action. It was time again for Power-Point. Gardiner displayed a map of Iran, with stars indicating the facilities known or believed to be involved in some way in the country's nuclear programs. The stars were spattered across the country, north to south and east to west. Then he put up a map showing the route Israeli warplanes would have to take in order to reach some or all of the sites. Osirak, in Iraq, had by comparison been practically next door, and the Israeli warplanes had made the round trip without refueling. To get to Iran, Israeli planes would have to fly over Saudi Arabia and Jordan, probably a casus belli in itself given current political conditions; or over Turkey, also a problem; or over American-controlled Iraq, which would require (and signal) U.S. approval of the mission.

With this the DCI left the podium—and Sam Gardiner, now sitting at the table as national security adviser, asked what initial assessments the principals made of the Iranian threat.

On one point there was concord. Despite Gardiner's emphasis on the tentative nature of the intelligence, the principals said it was sufficient to demonstrate the gravity of the threat. David Kay, a real-life nuclear inspector who was now the DCI at the table, said that comparisons with Iraq were important—and underscored how difficult the Iranian problem would be. "It needs to be emphasized," he said, "that the bases for conclusions about Iran are different, and we think stronger than they were with regard to Iraq." He explained that international inspectors withdrew from Iraq in 1998, so outsiders had suspicions rather than hard knowledge about what was happening. In Iran inspectors had been present throughout, and had seen evidence of the "clandestine and very difficult-to-penetrate nature of the program," which "leaves no doubt that it is designed for a nuclear-weapons program." What is worse, he said, "this is a lot more dangerous than the Iraqi program, in that the Iranians have proven, demonstrated connections with very vicious international terrorist regimes who have shown their willingness to use any weapons they acquire" against the United States and its allies. Others spoke in the same vein.

The real debate concerned Israel. The less America worried about reaction from Europe and the Muslim world, the more likely it was to encourage or condone Israeli action, in the hope that Israel could solve the problem on its own. The more it worried about long-term relations with the Arab world, the more determined it would be to discourage the Israelis from acting.

Most of the principals thought the Israelis were bluffing, and that their real goal was to put pressure on the United States to act. "It's hard to fault them for making this threat," said Pollack, as the Democratic secretary of state, "because in the absence of Israeli pressure how seriously would the United States be considering this option? Based on my discussions with the Israelis, I think they know they don't have the technical expertise to deal with this problem. I think they know they just don't have the planes to get there—setting aside every other problem."

"They might be able to get there—the problem would be getting home," retorted Gerecht, who had the most positive view on the usefulness of an Israeli strike.

Bacon, as White House chief of staff, said, "Unless they can take out every single Iranian missile, they know they will get a relatively swift counterattack, perhaps with chemical weapons. So the threat they want to eliminate won't be eliminated." Both he and Pollack recommended that the administration ask the Israelis to pipe down.

"There are two things we've got to remember with regard to the Israelis," Kay said. "First of all, if we tell them anything, they are certain to play it back through their network that we are 'bringing pressure to bear' on them. That has been a traditional Israeli response. It's the nature of a free democracy that they will do that. The second thing we've got to be careful of and might talk to the Israelis about: our intelligence estimate that we have three years to operate could change if the Iranians thought the Israelis might preempt sooner. We'd like to have that full three years, if not more. So when we're talking with the Israelis, toning down their rhetoric can be described as a means of dealing with the threat."

Woven in and out of this discussion was a parallel consideration of Iraq: whether, and how, Iran might undermine America's interests there or target its troops. Pollack said this was of great concern. "We have an enormous commitment to Iraq, and we can't afford to allow Iraq to fail," he said. "One of the interesting things that I'm going to ask the CentCom commander when we hear his presentation is, can he maintain even the current level of security in Iraq, which of course is absolutely dismal, and still have the troops available for anything in Iran?" As it happened, the question never came up in just this form in the stage of the game that featured a simulated CentCom commander. But Pollack's concern about the strain on U.S. military resources was shared by the other panelists. "The second side of the problem," Pollack continued, "is that one of the things we have going for us in Iraq, if I can use that term, is that the Iranians really have not made a major effort to thwart us . . . If they wanted to make our lives rough in Iraq, they could make Iraq hell." Provoking Iran in any way, therefore, could mean even fewer troops to handle Iraq—and even worse problems for them to deal with.

Kay agreed. "They may decide that a bloody defeat for the United States, even if it means chaos in Iraq, is something they actually would prefer. Iranians are a terribly strategic political culture . . . They might well accelerate their destabilization operation, in the belief that their best reply to us is to ensure that we have to go to helicopters and evacuate the Green Zone."

More views were heard—Gerecht commented, for example, on the impossibility of knowing the real intentions of the Iranian government—before Gardiner called a halt to this first phase of the exercise. He asked for a vote on one specific recommendation to the president: Should the United States encourage or discourage Israel in its threat to strike? The secretary of defense, the DCI, the White House chief of staff, and Secretary of State Pollack urged strong pressure on Israel to back off. "The threat of Israeli military action both harms us and harms our ability to get others to take courses of action that might indeed affect the Iranians," Kay said. "Every time a European hears that the Israelis are planning an Osirak-type action, it makes it harder to get their cooperation." Secretary of State Gerecht thought a successful attack was probably beyond Israel's technical capability, but that the United States should not publicly criticize or disagree with its best ally in the Middle East.

Sam Gardiner took the podium again. Now he was four-star General Gardiner, commander of CentCom. The president wanted to understand the options he actually had for a military approach to Iran. The general and his staff had prepared plans for three escalating levels of involvement: a punitive raid against key Revolutionary Guard units, to retaliate for Iranian actions elsewhere, most likely in Iraq; a preemptive air strike on possible nuclear facilities; and a "regime-change" operation, involving the forcible removal of the mullahs' government in Tehran. Either of the first two could be done on its own, but the third would require the first two as preparatory steps. In the real world the second option—a preemptive air strike against Iranian nuclear sites—is the one most often discussed. Gardiner said that in his briefing as war-game leader he would present versions of all three plans based as closely as possible on current military thinking. He would then ask the principals to recommend not that an attack be launched but that the president authorize the preparatory steps to make all three possible.

The first option was straightforward and, according to Gardiner, low-risk. The United States knew where the Revolutionary Guard units were, and it knew how to attack them. "We will use Stealth airplanes, U.S.–based B-2 bombers, and cruise missiles to attack," Gardiner said. "We could do this in one night." These strikes on military units would not in themselves do anything about Iran's nuclear program. Gardiner mentioned them because they would be a necessary first step in laying the groundwork for the ultimate scenario of forced regime change, and because they would offer the United States a "measured" retaliatory option if Iran were proved to be encouraging disorder in Iraq.

The preemptive air strike was the same one that had been deemed too demanding for the Israelis. The general's staff had identified 300 "aim points" in Iran. Some 125 of them were sites thought to be involved in producing nuclear, chemical, or biological weapons. The rest were part of Iran's air-defense or command system. "I call this a low-risk option also," Gardiner said, speaking for CentCom. "I'm not doing that as political risk—that's your job. I mean it's a low-risk military option." Gardiner said this plan would start with an attack on air-defense sites and would take five days in all.

Then there was option No. 3. Gardiner called this plan "moderate risk," but said the best judgment of the military was that it would succeed. To explain it he spent thirty minutes presenting the very sorts of slides most likely to impress civilians: those with sweeping arrows indicating the rapid movement of men across terrain. (When the exercise was over, I told David Kay that an observer who had not often seen such charts remarked on how "cool" they looked. "Yes, and the longer you've been around, the more you learn to be skeptical of the 'cool' factor in PowerPoint," Kay said. "I don't think the president had seen many charts like that before," he added, referring to President Bush as he reviewed war plans for Iraq.)

The overall plan of attack was this: a "deception" effort from the south, to distract Iranian troops; a main-force assault across the long border with Iraq; airborne and Special Forces attacks from Afghanistan and Azerbaijan; and cruise missiles from ships at sea. Gardiner presented more detailed possibilities for the deployment. A relatively "light" assault would involve two or three U.S. divisions attacking Iran on one front. The main U.S. force would come from existing bases in Iraq across the border into the western reaches of Iran. Their efforts would be augmented by special forces operators who had worked their way into other corners of the country. A "heavier" assault would mean larger numbers of troops and machines striking simultaneously on two fronts: into western Iran, from Iraq, and into southern Iran, from forces at various points in and around the Persian Gulf.

In all their variety, these and other regime-change plans he described had two factors in common. One is that they minimized "stability" efforts—everything that would happen after the capital fell. "We want to take out of this operation what has caused us problems in Iraq," Gardiner of CentCom said, referring to the postwar morass. "The idea is to give the president an option that he can execute that will involve about twenty days of buildup that will probably not be seen by the world. Thirty days of operation to regime change and taking down the nuclear system, and little or no stability operations. Our objective is to be on the outskirts of Tehran in about two weeks. The notion is we will not have a Battle of Tehran; we don't want to do that. We want to have a battle around the city. We want to bring our combat power to the vicinity of Tehran and use Special Operations to take the targets inside the capital. We have no intention of getting bogged down in stability operations in Iran afterward. Go in quickly, change the regime, find a replacement, and get out quickly after having destroyed—rendered inoperative—the nuclear facilities." How could the military dare suggest such a plan, after the disastrous consequences of ignoring "stability" responsibilities in Iraq? Even now, Gardiner said after the war game, the military sees postconflict operations as peripheral to its duties. If these jobs need to be done, someone else must take responsibility for them.

The other common factor was the need for troops, machinery, and weapons to be nearby and ready to move. Positioning troops would not be that big a problem. When one unit was replacing another in Iraq, for a while both units would be in place, and the attack could happen then. But getting enough machinery into place was more complicated, because airfields in nearby Georgia and Azerbaijan are too small to handle a large flow of military cargo planes.

As CentCom commander, Gardiner cautioned that any of the measures against Iran would carry strategic risks. The two major dangers were that Iran would use its influence to inflame anti-American violence in Iraq, and that it would use its leverage to jack up oil prices, hurting America's economy and the world's. In this sense option No. 2—the preemptive air raid—would pose as much risk as the full assault, he said. In either case the Iranian regime would conclude that America was bent on its destruction, and it would have no reason to hold back on any tool of retaliation it could find. "The region is like a mobile," he said. "Once an element is set in motion, it is impossible to say where the whole thing will come to rest." But the president had asked for a full range of military options, and unless his closest advisers were willing to go to him empty-handed, they needed to approve the steps that would keep all the possibilities alive. That meant authorizing the Department of Defense to begin expanding airfields, mainly in Azerbaijan, and to dedicate $700 million to that purpose. (As it happens, this is the same amount Tommy Franks requested in July 2002, to keep open the possibility of war in Iraq.) "This is not about executing the plan," Gardiner of CentCom said. "We're preparing options for the president; the whole issue of execution is separate. We need some money to build facilities."

Gardiner remained at the podium to answer questions as the CentCom commander, and the discussion began. The panelists skipped immediately to the regime-change option, and about it there was unanimity: the plan had been modeled carefully on the real assault on Iraq, and all five advisers were appalled by it.

"You need to take this back to Tampa," David Kay said, to open the discussion. Tampa, of course, is the headquarters for CentCom units operating in Iraq and Afghanistan. "Or put it someplace else I'd suggest, but we're in public." What was remarkable about the briefing, he said, was all the charts that were not there. "What were the countermoves?"

he asked. "The military countermoves—not the political ones you off-loaded to my secretaries of state but the obvious military countermoves that the Iranians have? A very easy military counter is to raise the cost of your military operation inside Iraq. Are you prepared to do that?"

The deeper problem, Kay said, lay with the request for money to "keep options open." "That, quite frankly, is a bunch of bullshit," he said. "Approval of the further planning process forecloses a number of options immediately. I would love to see a strategic communications plan that would allow us to continue diplomatic and other options immediately with our European allies when this leaks; inevitably this will leak."

The next twenty minutes of discussion was to the same effect. Who, exactly, would succeed the mullahs in command? How on earth would U.S. troops get out as quickly as they had come in? "Speaking as the president's chief of staff, I think you are doing the president an enormous disservice," Kenneth Bacon said. "One, it will leak. Two, it will be politically and diplomatically disastrous when it leaks . . . I think your invasion plan is a dangerous plan even to have on the table in the position of being leaked . . . I would throw it into Tampa Bay and hope the sharks would eat it."

"This is a paranoid regime," Kenneth Pollack said of Iran. "Even if the development of the Caucasus airfields . . . even if it weren't about them, they would assume it was about them. So that in and of itself will likely provoke a response. The Iranians are not inert targets! If they started to think we were moving in the direction of a military move against them, they would start fighting us right away."

Michael Mazarr, as secretary of defense, said he did not want the authority that was on offer to his department. "Tell the president my personal judgment would be the only circumstances in which we could possibly consider launching any significant operation in Iran would be the most extreme provocation, the most imminent threat," he said.

Even the hardest-liner, Reuel Gerecht, was critical. "I would agree that our problems with the Islamic republic will not be over until the regime is changed," he said. If the United States could launch a genuine surprise attack— suddenly, from aircraft carriers, rather than after a months-long buildup of surrounding airfields—he would look at it favorably. But on practical grounds, he said, "I would vote against the regime-change options displayed here."

Further unhappy back-and-forth ensued, with the Cent-Com commander defending the importance of keeping all options open, and the principals warning of trouble when news of the plan got out. When Gardiner called an end to this segment, there was little objection to the most modest of the military proposals—being ready, if need be, for a punitive strike on the Revolutionary Guards. The participants touched only briefly on the Osirak-style strike during the war game, but afterward most of them expressed doubt about its feasibility. The United States simply knew too little about which nuclear projects were under way and where they could be destroyed with confidence. If it launched an attack and removed some unknown proportion of the facilities, the United States might retard Iran's progress by an unknown number of months or years—at the cost of inviting all-out Iranian retaliation. "Preemption is only a tactic that puts off the nuclear development," Gardiner said after the exercise. "It cannot make it go away. Since our intelligence is so limited, we won't even know what we achieved after an attack. If we set it back a year, what do we do a year later? A preemptive strike would carry low military risk but high strategic risk."

During the war game the regime-change plan got five nays. But it was clear to all that several other big issues lay on the table, unresolved. How could the president effectively negotiate with the Iranians if his own advisers concluded that he had no good military option to use as a threat? How could the world's most powerful and sophisticated military lack the ability to take an opponent by surprise? How could leaders of that military imagine, after Iraq, that they could ever again propose a "quick in-and-out" battle plan? Why was it so hard to develop plans that allowed for the possibility that an adversary would be clever and ruthless? Why was it so hard for the United States to predict the actions and vulnerabilities of a regime it had opposed for twenty-five years?

At noon the war game ended. As a simulation it had produced recommendations that the president send a go-slow signal to the Israelis and that he not authorize any work on airfields in Central Asia. His advisers recommended that he not even be shown CentCom's plans for invading Iran.

The three hours of this exercise were obviously not enough time for the panel of advisers to decide on all aspects of a new policy toward Iran. But the intended purpose of the exercise was to highlight the real options a real president might consider. What did it reveal? Gardiner called for a wrap-up from participants and observers immediately after the event. From their comments, plus interviews with the participants in the following week, three big themes emerged: the exercise demonstrated something about Iraq, something about the way governments make decisions, and something about Iran.

Iraq was a foreground topic throughout the game, since it was where a threatened Iran might most easily retaliate. It was even more powerful in its background role. Every aspect of discussion about Iran was colored by knowledge of how similar decisions had played out in Iraq. What the United States knew and didn't know about secret weapons projects. What could go wrong with its military plans. How much difficulty it might face in even a medium-size country. "Compared with Iraq, Iran has three times the population, four times the land area, and five times the problems," Kenneth Pollack said during the war game. A similar calculation could be heard in almost every discussion among the principals, including those who had strongly supported the war in Iraq. This was most obvious in the dismissal of the full-scale regime-change plan—which, Gardiner emphasized, was a reflection of real-life military thinking, not a straw man. "I have been working on these options for almost eighteen months," he said later. "I tried them in class with my military students. They were the best I could do. I was looking for a concept that would limit our involvement in stability operations. We just don't have the forces to do that in Iran. The two lesser concepts"—punitive raids on the Revolutionary Guard and preemptive air strikes—"were really quite good from a military perspective." And of course the sweeping third concept, in the very similar form of Tommy Franks's plan, had been approved by a real president without the cautionary example of Iraq to learn from.

Exactly what learning from Iraq will mean is important but impossible to say. "Iraq" could become shorthand for a comprehensive disaster—one of intention, execution, and effect. "Usually we don't make the same mistakes immediately," Graham Allison said. "We make different mistakes." In an attempt to avoid "another Iraq," in Iran or elsewhere, a different administration would no doubt make new mistakes. If George Bush is reelected, the lessons of Iraq in his second term will depend crucially on who is there to heed them. All second-term presidents have the same problem, "which is that the top guys are tired out and leave—or tired out and stay," Kay said. "You get the second-best and the second-brightest, it's really true." "There will be new people, and even the old ones will behave differently," Gardiner said. "The CIA will not make unequivocal statements. There will be more effort by everyone to question plans." But Kay said that the signal traits of the George W. Bush administration—a small group of key decision-makers, no fundamental challenge of prevailing views—would most likely persist. "I have come to the conclusion that it is a function of the way the president thinks, operates, declares his policy ahead of time," Kay said. "It is inherent in the nature of George Bush, and therefore inherent in the system."

What went wrong in Iraq, according to our participants, can in almost all cases be traced back to the way the administration made decisions. "Most people with detailed knowledge of Iraq, from the CIA to the State Department to the Brits, thought it was a crazy quilt held together in an artificial state," Allison said. Because no such people were involved in the decision to go to war, the administration expected a much easier reception than it met—with ruinous consequences. There was no strong institutional system for reconciling differences between the Pentagon, the State Department, the CIA, and other institutions, and the person who theoretically might have done this, Condoleezza Rice, was weak. "If you don't have a deliberate process in which the national security adviser is playing a strong role, clarifying contrary views, and hammering out points of difference, you have the situation you did," Allison said. "There was no analytic memo that all the parties looked at that said, 'Here's how we see the shape of this problem; here is the logic that leads to targeting Iraq rather than North Korea.'"

"Process" sounds dull, and even worse is "government decision-making," but these topics provoked the most impassioned comments from panelists and observers when they were interviewed after the war game. All were alarmed about the way governments now make life-and-death decisions; this was, after Iraq, the second big message of the exercise.

"Companies deciding which kind of toothpaste to market have much more rigorous, established decision-making processes to refer to than the most senior officials of the U.S. government deciding whether or not to go to war," Michael Mazarr said. "On average, the national-security apparatus of the United States makes decisions far less rigorously than it ought to, and is capable of. The Bush administration is more instinctual, more small-group-driven, less concerned about being sure they have covered every assumption, than other recent administrations, particularly that of George H. W. Bush. But the problem is bigger than one administration or set of decision-makers."

Gardiner pointed out how rare it is for political leaders to ask, "And what comes after that? And then?" Thomas Hammes, the Marine Corps expert in counterinsurgency, said that presentations by military planners feed this weakness in their civilian superiors, by assuming that the adversary will cooperate. "We never 'red-celled' the enemy in this exercise" (that is, let him have the first move), Hammes said after the Iran war game. "What if they try to preempt us? What if we threaten them, and the next day we find mines in Baltimore Harbor and the Golden Gate, with a warning that there will be more? Do we want to start this game?" Such a failure of imagination—which Hammes said is common in military-run war games—has a profound effect, because it leads to war plans like the ones from Gardiner's CentCom, or from Tommy Franks, which in turn lull presidents into false confidence. "There is no such thing as a quick, clean war," he said. "War will always take you in directions different from what you intended. The only guy in recent history who started a war and got what he intended was Bismarck," who achieved the unification of Germany after several European wars.

Gardiner pointed out that none of the principals had even bothered to ask whether Congress would play a part in the decision to go to war. "This game was consistent with a pattern I have been seeing in games for the past ten years," he said. "It is not the fault of the military, but they have learned to move faster than democracy was meant to move."

And what did the exercise show about Iran? In the week after the war game I interviewed the participants about the views they had expressed "in role" and about their personal recommendations for the next president's approach. From these conversations, and from the participants' other writings and statements about Iran, the following themes emerged.

About Iran's intentions there is no disagreement. Iran is trying to develop nuclear weapons, and unless its policy is changed by the incentives it is offered or the warnings it receives, it will succeed.

About America's military options there is almost as clear a view. In circumstances of all-out war the United States could mount an invasion of Iran if it had to. If sufficiently provoked—by evidence that Iran was involved in a terrorist incident, for example, or that it was fomenting violence in Iraq—the United States could probably be effective with a punitive bomb-and-missile attack on Revolutionary Guard units.

But for the purposes most likely to interest the next American president—that is, as a tool to slow or stop Iran's progress toward nuclear weaponry—the available military options are likely to fail in the long term. A full-scale "regime-change" operation has both obvious and hidden risks. The obvious ones are that the United States lacks enough manpower and equipment to take on Iran while still tied down in Iraq, and that domestic and international objections would be enormous. The most important hidden problem, exposed in the war-game discussions, was that a full assault would require such drawn-out preparations that the Iranian government would know months in advance what was coming. Its leaders would have every incentive to strike preemptively in their own defense. Unlike Saddam Hussein's Iraq, a threatened Iran would have many ways to harm America and its interests. Apart from cross-border disruptions in Iraq, it might form an outright alliance with al-Qaeda to support major new attacks within the United States. It could work with other oil producers to punish America economically. It could, as Hammes warned, apply the logic of "asymmetric" or "fourth-generation" warfare, in which a superficially weak adversary avoids a direct challenge to U.S. military power and instead strikes the most vulnerable points in American civilian society, as al-Qaeda did on 9/11. If it thought that the U.S. goal was to install a wholly new regime rather than to change the current regime's behavior, it would have no incentive for restraint.

What about a preemptive strike of our own, like the Osirak raid? The problem is that Iran's nuclear program is now much more advanced than Iraq's was at the time of the raid. Already the U.S. government has no way of knowing exactly how many sites Iran has, or how many it would be able to destroy, or how much time it would buy in doing so. Worse, it would have no way of predicting the long-term strategic impact of such a strike. A strike might delay by three years Iran's attainment of its goal—but at the cost of further embittering the regime and its people. Iran's intentions when it did get the bomb would be all the more hostile.

Here the United States faces what the military refers to as a "branches and sequels" decision—that is, an assessment of best and second-best outcomes. It would prefer that Iran never obtain nuclear weapons. But if Iran does, America would like Iran to see itself more or less as India does—as a regional power whose nuclear status symbolizes its strength relative to regional rivals, but whose very attainment of this position makes it more committed to defending the status quo. The United States would prefer, of course, that Iran not reach a new level of power with a vendetta against America. One of our panelists thought that a strike would help the United States, simply by buying time. The rest disagreed. Iran would rebuild after a strike, and from that point on it would be much more reluctant to be talked or bargained out of pursuing its goals—and it would have far more reason, once armed, to use nuclear weapons to America's detriment.

Most of our panelists felt that the case against a U.S. strike was all the more powerful against an Israeli strike. With its much smaller air force and much more limited freedom to use airspace, Israel would probably do even less "helpful" damage to Iranian sites. The hostile reaction—against both Israel and the United States—would be potentially more lethal to both Israel and its strongest backer.

A realistic awareness of these constraints will put the next president in an awkward position. In the end, according to our panelists, he should understand that he cannot prudently order an attack on Iran. But his chances of negotiating his way out of the situation will be greater if the Iranians don't know that. He will have to brandish the threat of a possible attack while offering the incentive of economic and diplomatic favors should Iran abandon its plans. "If you say there is no acceptable military option, then you end any possibility that there will be a nonnuclear Iran," David Kay said after the war game. "If the Iranians believe they will not suffer any harm, they will go right ahead." Hammes agreed: "The threat is always an important part of the negotiating process. But you want to fool the enemy, not fool yourself. You can't delude yourself into thinking you can do something you can't." Is it therefore irresponsible to say in public, as our participants did and we do here, that the United States has no military solution to the Iran problem? Hammes said no. Iran could not be sure that an American president, seeing what he considered to be clear provocation, would not strike. "You can never assume that just because a government knows something is unviable, it won't go ahead and do it. The Iraqis knew it was not viable to invade Iran, but they still did it. History shows that countries make very serious mistakes."

So this is how the war game turned out: with a finding that the next American president must, through bluff and patience, change the actions of a government whose motives he does not understand well, and over which his influence is limited. "After all this effort, I am left with two simple sentences for policymakers," Sam Gardiner said of his exercise. "You have no military solution for the issues of Iran. And you have to make diplomacy work."

AFTERWORD

In journalism you always learn things after publishing a story that you wish you'd known when you were writing it. That experience was stronger with this series of articles than with anything else I had written since entering the magazine world in the 1970s. As each article was published, I would receive telephone calls, letters, and most of all e-mail messages from people who had been involved in the decisions I was describing. Fortunately from my perspective, very rarely were these people writing to correct details or challenge conclusions in what I had written. Most of the time they offered their own complementary view of episodes I had described, and suggested anecdotes, contacts, or possibilities for future stories—many of which I later used.*

What I have learned through this network of new friends and informants parallels what I have observed in other journalistic, academic, and military reports on the war. While the ultimate outcome of events in Iraq is unknowable, the

---

*Of course, there is a potential selection bias in people who choose to write to the author of a story. Those with supporting details to offer might be more likely to write than those who are exasperated by the story's whole approach. But my past experience had taught me that people who are unhappy about a story rarely hesitate to let the author know. The *Atlantic* did not have to publish any correction or retraction about these articles.

following sequence of claims, related to the arguments developed in the preceding chapters, now seems to have been established beyond reasonable question:

The difficult consequences of invading and occupying Iraq should have been foreseeable; they were in fact foreseen by many branches of the U.S. government and their counterparts in other countries. For reasons that included ideological preconception, bureaucratic rivalry, the confusion of battle, and simple negligence and incompetence, most of the potentially useful preparatory work was ignored, overruled, or thrown away. As a result the decision to invade Iraq became far costlier, in both money and blood—to Americans, Iraqis, and others—than it needed to have been.

We cannot know how many of the regional and sectarian tensions of current postwar Iraq would have arisen even with the best-managed occupation. We cannot know exactly how different today's Iraq would be if occupying troops had quickly imposed public order, rather than letting looters reign for weeks; or if they had been accompanied by enough interpreters or Arabic-speaking allies to reduce the terrifying and embittering effect of their house-to-house raids; or if they had realized the disastrous symbolic potential of detaining thousands of suspects at the same Abu Ghraib prison that had been Saddam Hussein's torture center, and through either negligence or intention letting it become a site of abuse and torture again. It is also true that we cannot know how many more of his own people Saddam Hussein would have tortured or killed if he had remained in power, or if he would have funded al-Qaeda to attack America.

What we can say is this: the thoughtlessness and lack of care with which the United States carried out its campaign for Iraq, like the thoughtlessness and lack of care with which it has approached the broader effort against Islamic terrorism, is a shame for the country and a setback in America's effort to defend itself.

The thoughtlessness described in this book is baffling. The people with most at stake in a successful outcome in Iraq were those who had tied America's welfare and their own reputations, now and into history, to the hope that Iraq could be transformed into an open, democratic, multiethnic, tolerant state that in turn would be an example to the Middle East. These were people who, in directing the resources of the U.S. government, potentially commanded more military and economic power than any set of leaders in history. President Bush persuaded Congress and the public that regime change in Iraq was the necessary next step in response to the 9/11 attacks. By all indications, Vice President Cheney was even more committed to this course. Secretary of State Colin Powell is now said to have demurred in private, but in public he bolstered the case for war. So did National Security Advisor Condoleezza Rice, with her warnings that the United States did not want "the smoking gun to be a mushroom cloud." Deputy Secretary of Defense Paul Wolfowitz was most impassioned of all about the moral and practical imperative of bringing democracy to the Arab-Islamic world. His superior, Donald Rumsfeld, epitomized confidence in the outcome of any venture led by the U.S. military. The assured bearing of General Tommy Franks of the Army, as head of Central Command, and General Richard Myers of the Air Force, as chairman of the Joint Chiefs of Staff, suggested why Rumsfeld was so confident.

These leaders, with their supporters, subordinates, and allies throughout the government, had everything to gain both personally and ideologically from a successful transition in Iraq. They controlled the resources the transition would need to succeed. Apart from Iraqis themselves, these were the people who had most to lose from a mismanaged transition. And yet it was this same group of leaders who, through errors of omission and commission, let the occupation fail. On the basis of all available evidence, it appears that the very people who were most insistent on the need to invade Iraq were most negligent about what would happen next.

There are some hypotheses about why this should have been so. Perhaps, as mentioned in the introduction, those pushing hardest for war recognized that extensive planning for postwar contingencies would inevitably slow the whole process down. They may therefore have concluded: whatever the long-term problems turn out to be, we can deal with them later on. Perhaps the leaders of the administration were genuinely surprised by the tangles of postwar Iraq, as they were by the failure to discover nuclear or chemical weapons in Iraq. Perhaps this was a failure of imagination, like the one that allowed European leaders to drift into World War I without conceiving how gravely they all would suffer. Perhaps the mixture of personalities at the top of the administration skewed decisions in a particular way. Perhaps some other factor will prove to have been decisive, when historians and memoirists have had their say.

Someday the process that led America to war in Iraq, and that led Iraq to the brink of civil war, will be as fully explored and explained as other major decision-making episodes in American presidential history. John Kennedy's response during the Cuban Missile Crisis in 1962 is the classic, carefully studied example of a risky choice that turned out well. I suspect that the Bush team's handling of Iraq will be grouped not with those deliberations but with Kennedy's mishandling of the Bay of Pigs invasion one year earlier, or with Lyndon Johnson's steps toward escalation in Vietnam in the mid-1960s.

Someday, military historians will reveal what American commanders in Iraq were thinking when they saw looting all around them but did not intervene. Presidential scholars will decide whether this President Bush was well or ill served by the advisors and organizational structure he relied on through these years. Diplomatic analysts of the future will be able to say whether America's frustrations in Iraq led to an overreactive withdrawal from foreign entanglements of any sort, much as the wounds America suffered in Vietnam under Presidents Johnson and Nixon made it politically impossible for Nixon's successor, President Ford, to intervene against the Khmer Rouge genocide in Cambodia in 1975. Or they may be able to say, on the contrary, that the Iraq misadventure taught the United States the kinds of commitments it can sustain and the ones it must avoid. One way or another, future Americans will speak about the "Lessons of Iraq." We just can't tell what lessons those will be.

For now, with uncertainty about how the story of Iraq will finally turn out, and with many of the people who made the crucial choices still in office and not as free to talk as they will ultimately be, we are left with a series of other questions and implications to consider. Here are three questions that stay with me, as I look back on four years of reporting about how my nation went to war, and look ahead to the war's repercussions.

The first is: What will this war eventually do to, and for, the American military? For at least a decade after the fall of Saigon in 1975, the military was preoccupied with recovering from its trauma in Vietnam. There were the practical problems of attracting and training enough new troops, after the hard experience of Vietnam had driven people away and created a "hollow army." There was the intellectual and doctrinal challenge of learning from what had gone wrong on this battlefield and deciding what kinds of battles modern America could fight. Most consequential of all, there was the political and even ethical imperative of reestablishing bonds of trust within a military whose internal cohesion had been eroded—as well as those between that military and the population it was supposed to represent and defend. The first Gulf War in 1991 was important within the American military because it represented full recovery from the strains of a generation earlier.

In the eyes of the general public, the American military has escaped blame for what has gone wrong in Iraq. The biggest errors and missteps have been blamed on the military's civilian superiors. In most cases, as explained in the preceding chapters, the civilians do indeed deserve the blame.

But inside the military, many people understand that the

situation is not that simple. Civilians—Bush, Rumsfeld, Wolfowitz, Bremer—made some choices that turned out badly. But military professionals have been in charge of the war day by day. They operated the prison at Abu Ghraib. They conducted the nighttime raids where Iraqi civilians were rousted from their homes. They tried to fight an insurgency using tanks and attack gunships, despite long evidence that such an approach would only make the problem worse. When Nigel Aylwin-Foster, a brigadier general in the British Army, wrote a scathing article late in 2005 about U.S. failures in Iraq, he was mainly criticizing Americans in uniform.*

By 2006, a movement had developed within the military, especially the ground forces of the Army and Marine Corps, to learn from the setbacks in Iraq while there was still time to improve performance there—and to be better prepared for future counterinsurgency efforts. In February of that year, Lieutenant General Dave Petraeus of the Army, featured in the chapter "Why Iraq Has No Army," convened a special conference at the Army's Command and General Staff College, in Fort Leavenworth, Kansas, to consider fundamentally new tactics against insurgents. Three years into

---

*The article was published in *Military Review*, a journal of the Army's Command and General Staff College at Fort Leavenworth, Kansas. Lieutenant General Dave Petraeus had just taken command at Fort Leavenworth. His decision to authorize publication of the article in one of the army's most prestigious journals was taken as a sign of impending debate inside the army about the culpability for operational failures in Iraq.

the occupation of Iraq, service there was placing unsustainable stress on the active duty Army and Marine Corps, as well as the Reserves and National Guard. Though serious, the strain of combat could be reduced when the troops were brought home. The deeper strain, of fighting an ambiguous and in many ways unsuccessful war, is the one whose resolution really matters to the military. Its outcome will determine whether the professional fighting force becomes harder and more sophisticated through its experience in Iraq, or again used-up and demoralized.

The second question involves relations between Americans in uniform and the rest of the nation. As they looked back on Vietnam, young officers of the 1980s and 1990s often felt that their civilian superiors had misled them—but that their leaders in uniform had fallen short as well. *Dereliction of Duty*, a 1997 book about Vietnam by a young officer then teaching at West Point, argued that the commanding generals of the 1960s should have resigned in protest rather than support a strategy they knew could not succeed. The author of that book, H. R. McMaster, became an inspirational figure to a rising group of officers. Yet by the time McMaster had become an Army colonel and was commanding the Third Armored Cavalry Regiment in Iraq, the uniformed services were again headed by generals who had in effect become political allies of an administration. Tommy Franks, after retiring as head of Central Command, spoke at the Republican convention of 2004. During the run-up to the invasion of Iraq in 2003, every reporter covering the Pentagon heard military complaints about the civilian-designed timetable and strategy (as preceding chapters indicate). But throughout this time, chairman of the Joint Chiefs of Staff Richard Myers blandly endorsed every aspect of administration policy in his press conferences and speeches. The point is not that Myers or his successor Peter Pace should ever have spoken disrespectfully of decisions made by their commander in chief. But to many watching from lower down the chain of command, their example suggested that political loyalty counted for more than independent professional judgment at the military's top rank.

The military's relationship with ordinary civilians is, if anything, more complicated than its connection with civilian commanders. Nearly two generations after the end of the draft, America's volunteer military is superior to any force the nation has fielded before. No commander wants to deal with reluctant conscripts again. Every American now serving in harm's way at some point voluntarily chose military service. Many of them did not realize they would be serving in Iraq; many National Guardsmen and reservists did not imagine they would be plucked out of civilian life for sustained tours overseas. But because all troops have in some sense volunteered, the military is spared much of the internal and external friction of the draft army years.

The question is whether there is too little friction. The administration constantly says that the nation is "at war," but of course it is not. The tiny fraction of Americans who are in uniform have been very hard pressed in the years since 9/11. Thousands have been killed; tens of thousands injured; hundreds of thousands sent overseas for months on end. But in a nation of more than 300 million people, the share affected by military service is smaller than at any time in more than a century. The army is in a war; much of the country watches it on TV. Although many cities have been heavily affected by mobilization of their National Guard and Reserve units, and while awareness of the troops' sacrifice is strongest in areas with large military concentrations, compared with any past large-scale effort, the country as a whole has been left out of the war.

Everyone in the military is aware of this imbalance. Most feel proud, even superior, about the role they are playing. But they all recognize what everyone else is not doing. In practical terms, it would be hugely difficult to restore the draft. Roughly 4 million Americans turn eighteen each year. That is at least twenty times as many people as the military now enlists per year. Even allowing for those who are unable to serve for physical, mental, religious, or other reasons, and even allowing for future growth in what the military calls "end strength," or total troop levels, today's American military could not absorb more than a tiny fraction of the total manpower available. And if it were to take that small fraction via the draft, all the old Vietnam-era questions of unfairness and discrimination would return.

So the nation cannot draft its way out of the current predicament of a tiny professional military that withstands all the pressure that a vast civilian population is spared. In my experience through interviews over the years, members of the professional military are proud of meeting higher standards, and being made of sterner stuff, than ordinary civilians are. But especially when their combat missions become unpopular, or merely drop out of the headlines, they are aware of how empty the public's "support" of its troops can seem.

The third question involves accountability. The nation undertook a battle for largely idealistic reasons. A number of its leaders thought they could bring democracy to people who deserved it, or at least free those people from torture and oppression. Despite the idealism of their goals, the results were in most ways a failure. They were a failure in a limited sense, in the theater of Iraq, and they failed more grandly, in undercutting the longer, harder struggle against violent religious extremism.

The country failed because individuals who led it failed. They made the wrong choices; they did not learn or listen; they were fools. No one responsible for these errors was dismissed from the administration. No senior officer was relieved or reprimanded. After President Bush withstood what he called an "accountability moment" in the election of 2004, he promoted or decorated with medals the members of the team that had ill served the nation.

"Hindsight is not a strategy," President Bush said in his State of the Union address in 2006. But accountability, and any hope of learning from errors, requires an honest look back at what has occurred.

James Fallows
Washington, April 2006